Trams Around Dewsbury and Wakefield

TRANSPORT THROUGH THE AGES

Transport Through the Ages is a new and fascinating collection of transport titles, brought to you by Wharncliffe Books. This delightful series is intended to highlight the various modes of transport from the railways to the canals, exploring the transitional journey of their operation. These highly illustrated books, contain astounding pictures, spanning the last century, which captivate the history and nostalgia of the locality.

Other titles in the series:

Canals and River Section of The Aire and Calder Navigation
Mike Taylor
1-903425-37-9 . £9.99

Trams & Trolleybuses in Doncaster, Richard Buckley
1-903425-29-8 . £9.99

Barnsley Buses, Stephen Farnsworth and Roger Glister
1-871647-91-6 . £9.99

Other local books:

The Making of The West Yorkshire Landscape, Anthony Silson
1-903425-31-X . £9.99

Aspects of Huddersfield 2, Stephen Wade
1-903425-23-9 . £9.99

From Wakefield to Towton, Philip A. Haigh
0-85052-825-9 . £9.95

Aspects of Wakefield 3, Kate Taylor
1-903425-06-9 . £9.95

Aspects of Leeds 3, Lynne Stevenson Tate
1-903425-05-0 . £9.99

The Making of Huddersfield, Dr George Redmonds
1-903425-39-5 . £9.99

More Foul Deeds and Suspicious Deaths in Wakefield, Kate Taylor
1-903425-48-4 . £9.99

Please contact us via any of the methods below for more information or a catalogue.
WHARNCLIFFE BOOKS
47 Church Street, Barnsley, South Yorkshire, S70 2AS
Tel: 01226 734555 / 734222 Fax: 01226 734438
E-mail: enquiries@pen-and-sword.co.uk Website:www.wharncliffebooks.co.uk

TRAMS AROUND DEWSBURY & WAKEFIELD

Norman Ellis

Series Editor
Brian Elliott

Wharncliffe Books

First Published in 2004 by
Wharncliffe Books
an imprint of
Pen and Sword Books Limited,
47 Church Street, Barnsley,
South Yorkshire. S70 2AS

For up-to-date information on other titles produced under the Wharncliffe imprint, please telephone or write to:

Wharncliffe Books
FREEPOST
47 Church Street
Barnsley
South Yorkshire S70 2BR
Telephone (24 hours): 01226 734555

ISBN: 1-903425-40-9

A CIP catalogue record of this book is available from the British Library

Front Cover illustration: *Upper Kirkgate, Wakefield*
Back Cover illustration: *(upper) West Riding tramcar in Pontefract Market Place.*
(lower) Yorkshire Woollen tramcar awaits departure for Heckmondwike.

Printed in the United Kingdom by
CPI UK

CONTENTS

Assembling overhead wires on Leeds Road, Newton Bar, Wakefield, in 1904. *Postcard: E I Walker, Wakefield*

INTRODUCTION

The first, last and only time I boarded a Wakefield tram was in 1941, which may seem surprising because they ceased to operate nine years before. I had gone on an errand to the house of friends of my parents. These people were looking after an evacuee named Alan, who was a few years my junior. He led me to a tramcar body in the back garden. I gazed at it, boarded it, but made no attempt to reach its upper deck. This tramcar shell, which had become a garden shed and summer house, was languishing just to the west of the Wakefield to Leeds Road, midway between Outwood Church and Lofthouse Gate. Trams had traversed that road until 1932.

I remember riding on the Leeds tramcars to Roundhay Park or Temple Newsam. These journeys were only a means to an end, because my interest in trams was minimal. I left school, trained as a draughtsman, and developed an interest in archaeology and architecture. In the late 1960s, I read two books about tramways, written by J Joyce and entitled *Tramway Twilight* and *Tramway Heyday*. My affection for trams was kindled. I decided to collect old postcards and photographs which featured them. I was particularly keen to acquire pictures which were local to me, especially those featuring the Dewsbury, Wakefield and Ossett systems.

The heyday of my local trams, 1903 to 1934, approximated to the golden age of the picture postcard. Photographers, armed with cumbersome cameras and glass plates, frequently included the prestigious trams in their pictures. The images on the negatives were transferred to sensitized material with 'postcard' printed on the back. The cards were sent to friends or stored in albums.

Conceived by the Victorians and developed by the Edwardians, electric trams became status symbols of cities and towns, and were indispensible to all except the very rich and very poor. The shops, pub, park, place of work or even Aunt Polly's house, became more accessible. Because of their thorough craftsmanship, the tramcars eventually began to look dated whilst still roadworthy.

This book covers three company-operated tramway systems, with headquarters in Dewsbury, Wakefield and Ossett respectively. (The other electric tramway undertakings in West Yorkshire were municipally owned and run). The Yorkshire (Woollen District) Electric Tramways operated in and to the north, south and west of

Dewsbury. The area, with its ridges and valleys, was famous for heavy woollens. The Yorkshire (West Riding) Electric Tramways were centred on the City of Wakefield, administrative heart of the West Riding, but the company also operated a tramway in the Castleford, Normanton and Pontefract areas which was not joined to the Wakefield sections. Coal mining and textiles were the staple industries. The Dewsbury, Ossett & Soothill Nether Tramways connected the towns of Ossett and Dewsbury.

Together, the above three systems possessed the potential for inter-company running, but this never materialized. A journey from, say, Ravensthorpe to Leeds was possible by changing trams at Dewsbury, Ossett and Wakefield. In such cases, rail travel would probably have been preferable. Stiff competition existed between train and tram, the Great Northern Railway being particularly vulnerable.

In 1986, various postcards listed in the catalogue of a Scottish auction house caught my eye. They were described as being a photographic record of building the tram depot and laying the tram tracks in Wakefield. By post, I submitted some (high) bids for the various lots. I was successful with my offers and highly delighted with the cards when they arrived, even though they cost me an arm and a leg. Most of these rare pictures feature in the book.

The knock-down selling price for some of the obsolete Wakefield tramcars in 1932 was £55. In certain spheres, prices of the better photographic tram postcards have topped this. It is partly a reflection of the esteem with which tram enthusiasts and historians rate the cards. Postcards, especially those produced by small-scale photographers in limited numbers, can be a unique source of information. Only one copy of some of the images will have survived.

Most of the illustrations in this book, many of them previously unpublished, are from my collection, built up over the last thirty years. I have refrained from giving an abundance of technical data, which is available in other books. The trams are presented against a varied background of places and people, of streets and squares, of work and play.

CHAPTER 1

Beginnings

In the latter half of the nineteenth century, the developing areas around Dewsbury and Wakefield attracted various railway companies which were eager to secure a share of passenger and goods traffic. A comprehensive and competing network of lines was laid. Dewsbury acquired three stations, Wakefield two. The rails were also laid to the lesser towns and many of the evolving villages. Because some of the passenger stations were inconveniently sited, and as people were accustomed to walking, the inclination to 'leg-it' lived on.

Into the region came other forms of public transport, notably horse buses and wagonettes, plus horse and steam trams. It was, however, the electric trams – clean, newfangled and very adaptable to road conditions – which created competion for the railways, particularly where relatively short passenger journeys were concerned.

The Dewsbury, Batley & Birstal (sic) Tramway Company constructed a horse tramway from Dewsbury to Birstall in 1874-5. The single track, with passing loops, was opened in stages: Dewsbury to Batley on 25 July 1874, Batley to Carlinghow on 25 March 1875 and Carlinghow to Birstall on 23 June 1875. An extension to Gomersal was opened in the autumn of 1881. These areas of increasing population included mills and, around Gomersal, collieries. The company ran seven double-deck tramcars. Each car was pulled by two horses, drawn from a stud of forty, to allow for rest periods or sick animals. The horses were uncoupled at the termini and led round to the other end of the car.

Steam trials took place on the Dewsbury, Batley & Birstal Tramway during 1876 and 1878. In the latter year, the Board of Trade inspector, Colonel Hutchinson, checked the line, using a Kitson steam engine and a trailer car. Although the ensuing formalities were protracted, regular steam traction was introduced on 10 April 1880, this being the first on-street steam passenger tramway in England. For a time, horse and steam operated side by side. Eventually, a mainly ten minute service was provided by eleven Merryweather locomotives and fourteen trailer cars, some of these being former horse trailers.

The British Electric Traction Company (BET) began buying shares in the Dewsbury, Batley & Birstal Tramway Company, and secured control in 1902. With a view to converting to electric traction, it entered into agreements with several local authorities – Dewsbury Borough, Batley Borough and the Birkenshaw, Birstall and Gomersal Urban District Councils – which purchased their portions of the tramway and leased them back to the BET. This organisation registered a new company, the Yorkshire (Woollen District) Electric Tramways, to electrify, operate and expand the system.

Meanwhile, in Wakefield, five miles away, tramways had been considered but not built. In 1882, the Wakefield Tramways Company proposed a steam or cable operated tramway, single line with passing loops, from St Michael's Church, along Westgate, Little Westgate, Kirkgate, over Chantry Bridge and branching along the roads to Agbrigg and Sandal. The owners of properties in narrow Little Westgate, mainly shopkeepers, objected. Further protests came from the Justices of the Peace for the West Riding, who were responsible for maintaining the old Chantry Bridge.

Wakefield had been served by privately operated horse buses and wagonettes since the 1840s. In 1890, the Wakefield City & District Omnibus Company commenced operating horse buses in and around Wakefield. Amongst the directors were W H Kingswell, costumier, and F K Perkin, watchmaker. The company's registered office was at 36 Wood Street. The original stable and yard were at the corner of George Street and Thornhill Street. When these premises became unsuitable, a lease was taken on houses, outbuildings and stables in Lower York Street and Hope Street. In 1903, the fleet consisted of forty-six horses, seven double deck and five single deck buses. Areas covered were Lofthouse Gate via Outwood, Sandal (some journeys to Newmillerdam), Agbrigg, Horbury and Calder Grove. Services to Ardsley were discontinued in 1895, partly because of railway competition. The remaining services were gradually withdrawn in 1904-5, when the Yorkshire (West Riding) Electric Tramways Company started to run trams.

Dewsbury, Batley & Birstal steam engine, fleet number 7, and trailer car, number 12 or 13, are featured at the Northgate terminus in Dewsbury. To the left of the engine is the waiting room and parcels office. The engine was purchased from Merryweather in 1881. Without its casing, it would have resembled a small four-wheel steam locomotive with a chimney above a horizontal boiler. The Board of Trade stipulated that the machinery of these engines must be concealed, which explains the all-round metal sheeting. The fender plate at each end was meant to remove obstructions – and obviate the possibility of running over anyone. The copper condenser tubes, visible on top of the engine, turned much of the steam back to water and returned it to the feed-water tank, thus enabling the engine to operate all day with one change of water. Coal or anthracite was carried on an integral bunker. The Board of Trade insisted that the engines must be free from noise caused by chimney blast or the clatter of machinery. Smoke and steam emissions were a problem, resulting in complaints to Dewsbury and Batley Corporations. At a maximum speed of around 10 mph, the threat of road accidents was not high. *Postcard.*

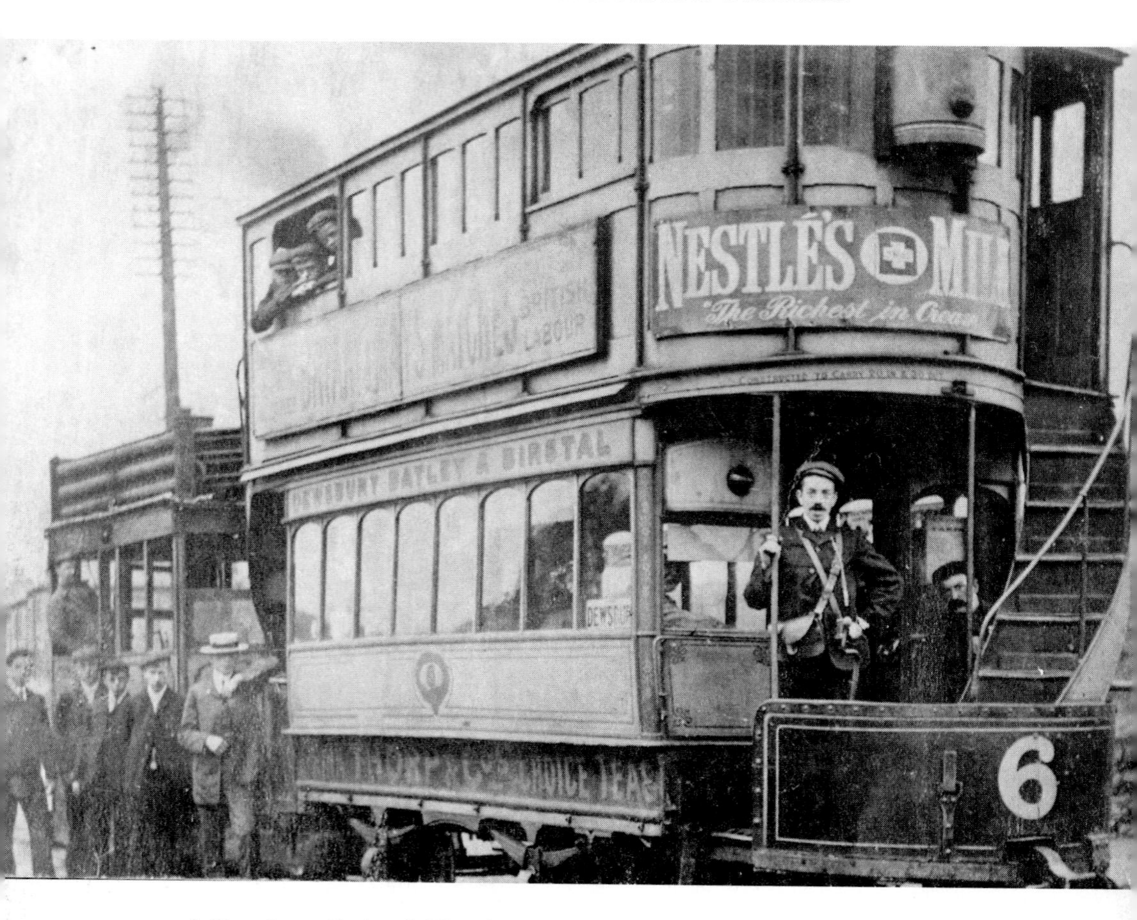

A Dewsbury, Batley & Birstal steam engine is shown with trailer car number 6 in its final form. (The company used the old spelling for Birstal with one l). Initially, the car was a horse trailer, without a roof over the upper deck, and seating for twenty on each level. When the car was rebuilt, an upper roof was added, to protect passengers from smoke fumes and inclement weather. The seating in the upper saloon was altered from knifeboard to transverse type and increased to thirty. The basic colour for trailers and engines is thought to have been bright chrome yellow, with lining out in darker colours. The engines originally were painted black or dark brown. *Postcard.*

A Wakefield City & District Omnibus Company bus is parked outside the Yorkshire Penny Bank in Westgate, Wakefield, prior to departure for Lofthouse Gate. The view, dating from 1904 (because the tram lines are visible) shows a twenty-six seat vehicle with three horses. The journey time to Lofthouse Gate was thirty-five minutes. In 1900, there were nine weekday journeys to and from Lofthouse Gate, with an extra journey in each direction on Saturdays. Timetables were published in local newspapers but not always adhered to because of driver inexperience, vagaries of horses and their occasional unavailability at relief points. *Postcard.*

Beside its terminus at the *Castle Inn*, Sandal, in 1904, is a Wakefield City & District Omnibus Company horse bus. Passengers are seated on the upper-deck crossbench seats; the inward facing lower-deck seats are occupied by a solitary passenger. A letter box is attached to the rear stairway. One of the decency boards (ladies were expected to conceal their legs) carries an advert for T P Braithwaite of the Crown Press, opposite the old *Six Chimneys* in Kirkgate, Wakefield. *Postcard.*

CHAPTER 2

Yorkshire (Woollen District) Electric Tramways Co Ltd

By 1900, the area to the west and north of Dewsbury had become a large heavily-populated conurbation of merging towns and villages, which were dependent on the textile industry, and particularly heavy woollens. Cleckheaton, Liversedge and Heckmondwike had developed near the course of the River Spen. Two railway companies – the Lancashire & Yorkshire and the London & North Western – had helped to generate the prosperity. Further south, Ravensthorpe had become an industrial suburb of thriving milltown Dewsbury, thanks to the River Calder, Calder & Hebble Navigation and the later railways. North of Dewsbury, Batley had grown into a flourishing milltown, being especially famous for reclaimed woollen products known as mungo and shoddy. Although the whole area was well-served by railways, the locations of many of the passenger stations did not suit everyone. A more passenger-friendly form of transportation was needed; electric trams seemed to be the answer. A municipal scheme was not practical, so a company-operated tramway was delivered.

The British Electric Traction Company was formed in 1895 to buy up existing horse and steam lines and promote electric tramways in Britain. It deposited plans for the *Spen Valley Light Railway Order* in 1899 and 1900. After their approval, the BET registered the Yorkshire (Woollen District) Electric Tramways Company on 19 November 1901.

Contractors for the permanent way and overhead equipment were Dick, Kerr & Company of Preston. A mixture of double track and single track (with passing loops) was laid, the latter being particularly evident in outlying areas. The overhead wires were suspended from side poles with bracket arms or from span wires. Much argument ensued as to which type of setts should be laid. The tram sheds at Frost Hill, Liversedge, and Savile Town, Dewsbury, were built by Drake & Garforth Brothers. The tramcars came from a variety of sources, although Brush of Loughborough featured prominently in their supply.

The first line to be inspected ran south from Dewsbury through Savile Town and Thornhill Lees, then east to Thornhill. On 18 February 1903, two double-deck cars left Savile Town depot and conveyed various officials along the route. Members of Thornhill Urban District Council drew the attention of Major Druitt, Board of Trade Inspector, to a dangerous curve where Brewery Lane met Lees Hall Road. He placed a 2 mph speed restriction on the sharp corner. Using single-deck cars because of low bridges, the Ravensthorpe route was then inspected as far as the Lancashire & Yorkshire railway bridge at the foot of Scout Hill. The party returned to Dewsbury Market Place, where double-deck cars were again boarded for an inspection of the Halifax Road route as far as the *Shoulder of Mutton Inn*. In his report, Major Druitt, although generally satisfied, made a number of stipulations with regard to speed. The Dewsbury to Thornhill route was opened to passengers on the same day as the inspection, Dewsbury to Ravensthorpe on 15 March 1903 and Dewsbury to the *Shoulder of Mutton* on 18 April.

Problems arose with construction and operation of the trunk line of the Yorkshire Woollen District (YWD) system, stretching from Dewsbury, through Heckmondwike, Liversedge and Cleckheaton to Moorend. A portion of proposed track along Halifax Road at Staincliffe lay within the Batley boundary and Batley Corporation wished to operate its own tramways. The YWD company had entered into agreements with all the relative local authorities except Batley, which stubbornly refused to co-operate. As a result, the Heckmondwike to Moorend section was inspected and opened on 24 April 1903, but it was 29 July before trams ran through from Dewsbury to Moorend.

The feud between Batley Corporation and the British Electric Traction Company had begun in 1900. The *Batley Corporation Tramways Order* 1900 was for a circular route from Hick Lane, taking in Wellington Street, Purlwell Lane, Track Road, Halifax Road, Healey Lane and Commercial Street. One branch would then go to Batley Market Place, the other would run along Branch Road to join the existing Bradford Road tramway. The corporation also wished to buy, electrify and operate a portion of the steam tramway in Bradford Road (by then belonging to the BET). The dispute was taken before the House of Lords in 1903. Meanwhile, to consolidate its position, Batley Corporation ordered eight tramcars. Then a wrangle arose over the supply of electric power.

Some common sense eventually prevailed. Batley Corporation constructed its circular route, much of it being single track with passing loops. However, in Halifax Road, double track was laid. Here, one set of track was owned by the company, the other by the corporation. But terms were agreed for leasing Batley Corporation's part of the tramway to the BET for twenty-eight years. In effect, this meant that the YWD operated the whole system. The official inspection of the circular route was arranged for 28 July 1903. Some alterations, requested by Major Druitt, had to be incorporated, and the circular passenger service was not inaugurated until 26 October 1903, after delivery of the corporation's eight tramcars. These were leased to the BET. The work of converting the steam tramway to electric power was completed in 1905. It included the conversion of the old steam tram depot at Carlinghow.

The year 1903 had seen the opening to passengers of the line from Liversedge to Hightown, plus the remainder of the Ravensthorpe line to Fir Cottage, each on 29 July. The Liversedge to Birkenshaw route was inspected and opened on 13 October 1903. The Yorkshire Woollen system altogether covered 22½ miles of route. This included 6¼ miles owned by Batley Corporation, and smaller sections owned by other local authorities. Steep gradients were a problem, but accidents were not common.

The number of tramcars operated by the YWD (including the eight Batley trams) totalled 82, the majority dating from the 1902-05 period. Single-deck and double-deck cars were run, all the latter initially having open tops. Within a short time, the fitting of top covers was implemented. With rebuilds, modifications, half-cars being spliced together and the purchase of secondhand Sheffield Corporation tramcars, the Yorkshire (Woollen District) fleet became interestingly varied.

Worn track, imminently expiring leases, greater reliability of motorbuses – all these were factors of the decision in the early 1930s to abandon the YWD tramways. The final section to close was the trunk route from Dewsbury to Cleckheaton. The last tram left Dewsbury during the late evening of 31 October 1934, with the Mayor of Dewsbury at the controls. The company, already an operator of motorbuses, changed its name to the Yorkshire Woollen District Transport Company Limited in 1935, and became one of the most successful bus operators in the BET group.

This 1902 scene shows tram lines being laid in Brewery Lane, Thornhill Lees. This was the first route to be opened by the Yorkshire (Woollen District) Electric Tramways Company. In the middle distance, right, a branch of the Dewsbury Pioneers' Industrial Society is just visible. Most of the work is being carried out further along the road, near the approach to Thornhill Station. The two boys, left, may have collected the trunk they are carrying from there. *Postcard: Kilner Goldsbrough.*

YWD tramcar number 18 is standing at Thornhill terminus, near the entrance to Combs Colliery, about two miles south of Dewsbury, in 1905. Its sole upper-deck passenger (a male) seems only vaguely interested in the bonny lasses taking part in the Whit Procession of Thornhill Parish Church. *Postcard.*

The tramway depot at Frost Hill, Liversedge, is seen almost complete in 1903. To the left, the administrative buildings are visible; to the right the actual sheds. Beyond the gateway, the single track fanned into ten sets of tracks, one set entering each of the ten bays, shown numbered 1 to 10. The featured tram, number 37, formed part of the company's first batch of double-deckers, fleet numbers 7 to 48, delivered in 1902-03. *Postcard: Herbert Jackson, photographer, Cleckheaton.*

The Market Place, Dewsbury, served as a tramway centre. Yorkshire Woollen District tramcars used its west side (actually on part of Northgate/Westgate). Dewsbury & Ossett trams terminated at its eastern extremity (near the Town Hall). Shortly after the opening of the tramway, the two tracks on the west side were increased to three. This photograph, from a card posted in August 1906, shows tramcar number 8 on the westernmost track, awaiting departure for Thornhill. Tramcar number 32, on the easternmost of the three tracks, is about to leave for Cleckheaton. Both these cars were part of the first batch of open-top double-deckers, numbers 7-48, delivered from Brush of Loughborough in 1902-03. The YWD started to fit top-deck covers within a year; those depicted were placed within the existing upper-deck sides. Number 32 shows its original wire mesh lifeguard, whereas number 8 has acquired a gate-and-tray type. The partly visible open-topped car appears to be number 40. The tramcars were painted crimson lake and cream, with lining out. The fleet number on either side of the headlamp was an arrangement adopted by several BET companies. On the corner leading into Market Place proper, three public houses are visible – the *Man & Saddle*, *King's Arms* and *Black Bull*. Behind the trams is the clock tower of Dewsbury Pioneers' Industrial Society. *Postcard: Fred Hartley, printer and photographer, Northgate, Dewsbury*

This view below of Market Place, Dewsbury, was probably captured in May or June 1910. It features YWD tramcars numbers 5 and 33 on the two outer tracks (of three). Single-deck car number 5 is awaiting departure for Fir Cottage, Ravensthorpe, whilst number 33 will shortly leave for Cleckheaton. The single-decker was part of the 1-6 batch delivered from Brush in 1902, partly for use on the Ravensthorpe route, where two low railway bridges made them necessary. Tramcars from both Ravensthorpe and Thornhill used the westernmost track, the trolley booms being swung round for the return journeys. Tramcars from Cleckheaton were similarly treated on the easternmost track. The centre track provided a through way for trams travelling to or from Savile Town Depot. As will be seen from this and the previous shot, advertising was allowed on the tramcars to provide extra revenue, although space was limited on the single-deckers. The imposing and still extant building on the left then housed the London City & Midland Bank. Beyond the single-deck tram can be seen the Dewsbury Coffee Tavern, now the site of Marks & Spencer. *Postcard.*

The three-track layout and a crossover are visible in this view of Westgate and Northgate (in the distance) at the edge of Dewsbury Market Place. The foremost horse-drawn cart appears to be gliding along one set of track, whilst an overcoated inspector wonders where all his trams have gone! *Postcard: WHS 'Kingsway' real photo series, number S 6606.*

Tramcar number 30, having just arrived from Thornhill, stands in Westgate, slightly short of its terminus in Dewsbury Market Place, awaiting departure of the single-decker in the distance. Its destination indicator has been changed to Combs Pit, ready for the return journey on the other track, gained via the crossover. *Postcard: S Dawson & Son, bookseller, Corporation Street, Dewsbury.*

Thornhill-bound tramcars, also those heading for Savile Town depot, had to cross the River Calder by Savile Bridge. Here, negotiating the bridge in about 1907, are a pair of similar, but not identical cars from the 7-48 batch. The one on the right has acquired a slightly later type of top cover, with a deeper wooden strip above the upstairs windows. *Postcard.*

These tramcars from the 7-48 batch are shown traversing the single track (with passing loops) of Lees Hall Road, Thornhill Lees, in about 1907. The white disc on the tram standard indicates a fare stage. *Postcard.*

Ready for the return run to Dewsbury, YWD tramcar number 26 waits at Thornhill terminus. The deeper wooden strip above the upstairs windows (mentioned earlier) is visible, as is the upper-deck sliding door. The earlier top covers had incorporated hinged doors. The practice of placing the fleet number on either side of the headlamp had been abandoned.
Photograph

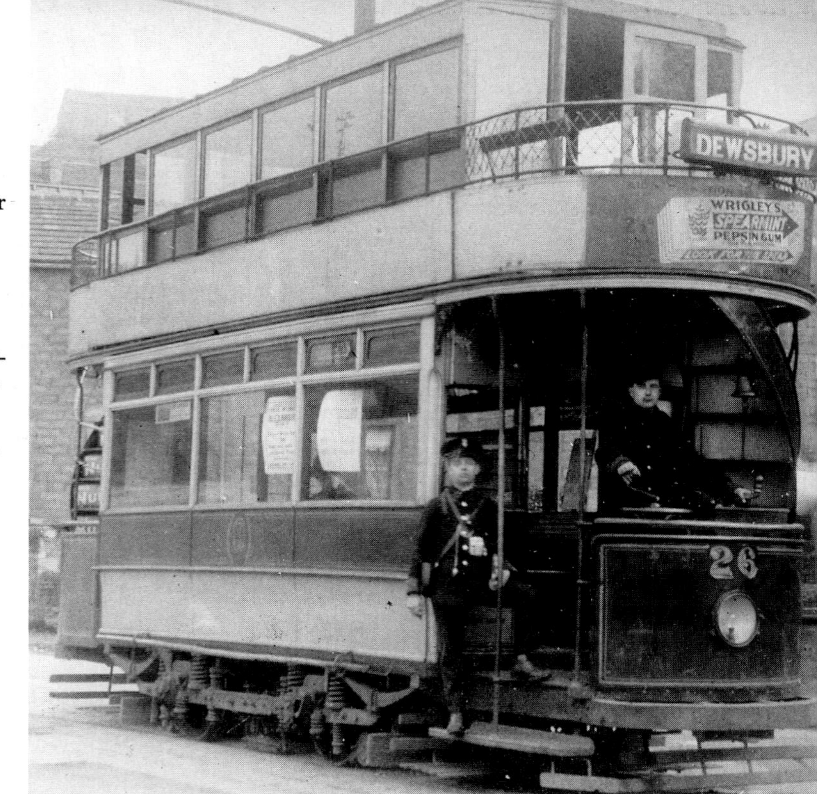

The driver and conductor of tramcar number 18 pose for the camera at Thornhill terminus, having just arrived from Dewsbury. The shaded headlamp suggests that this photograph was taken during the 1914-18 War. The tram incorporates an improved type of top cover, with five windows per side. *Postcard.*

A single-deck car of the Yorkshire Woollen 1-6 batch, new in 1902 and viewed here a couple of years later, has just left the terminus at Ravensthorpe Fir Cottage, and glided past the *Bull's Head Inn*, on its way back to Dewsbury. Single track, with passing loops, was considered adequate along much of this route. *Postcard.*

This later view shows the built-up part of Ravensthorpe, nearer to Dewsbury. Side poles and span wires are featured, as is the single track, which runs into a passing loop in the near distance. *Postcard: Allen & Sons, Oldham & Blackpool, number 457.*

Passenger traffic on the Ravensthorpe tramcar route soon built up. In 1903, this led to the purchase from Brush of two further single-deck cars, numbers 57-58, similar to those in the 1-6 batch. The illustration shows a well-wrapped driver and conductor who have positioned themselves on car number 57 at Ravensthorpe terminus, about 1910. The two later cars had straight-topped windows, whereas the earlier batch had elliptically-topped ones. Tramcars 57-58 seated thirty passengers on inward-facing longitudinal seats. The 1-6 batch had been delivered with two-and-one transverse seating. Before entering service, this was altered to longitudinal type. Thus, the two batches were comparable if not identical. *Postcard.*

Heavy Damages Against the Dewsbury Tramways Company

Judge Gent and a jury occupied a considerable time at Dewsbury on Thursday, on hearing a claim brought by Edward Littlewood, miner, Middle Road, Daw Green, for £500, for injuries to his son, who is five years of age, through the negligence of the Yorkshire (Woollen District) Electric Tramways Company. Mr C A Ridgway, for the plaintiff, said that on the 8th March, the child was crossing Huddersfield Road, near the points at the top of Webster Hill, Dewsbury, to join other children, who were listening to a street organ, when he was knocked down by a tramcar. His left foot was nearly torn off, and the leg had eventually to be amputated just below the knee. Thomas Ford and Joseph Dunford were eye witnesses of the accident. Ford twice shouted to the driver of the car, but he did not take the slightest notice or ring his bell. Ford, in his evidence, stated that after he shouted the first time the driver had sufficient time to pull up and prevent the accident. Mr T R D Wright, for the company, contended that it was a pure accident, and called evidence to show that the driver did not see the child until after the accident. He also said he was only travelling at the rate of a mile per hour when the accident occurred, and he could have brought the car to a standstill in a space of three feet. As he did not see the child before the accident, he had no chance to ring his bell. A verdict was given for the plaintiff, and the jury assessed the damages at £350.

Newspaper: *Ossett Observer,* 13 October 1906

A Little Girl's Terrible Death

A shocking fatal accident occurred at Scout Hill, Dewsbury, on Saturday afternoon. A little girl named Elsie Kershaw, the four year old daughter of Amy Kershaw, Albion Street, Ravensthorpe was playing with two other children. A tramcar was coming down Scout Hill, and deceased started to run across the tram lines. She was caught by the car, pulled underneath, and dragged for a distance of 45 yards before the car could be pulled up. It was then found she had been run over by two wheels and was dead, having sustained injuries to the head and face, whilst she was also disembowelled.

Newspaper: *Ossett Observer,* 14 April 1906

Pride of the Yorkshire (Woollen District) Electric Tramways was the route from Dewsbury to Cleckheaton Moorend. The stretch between Dewsbury and Liversedge was double track. In this illustration, beside the *Shoulder of Mutton Inn* on Halifax Road, Batley Carr, the two sets of track are seen rising up the steepest gradient (1in 8) of the route – and indeed the whole system. *Postcard.*

This busy scene, on a card posted in 1907, shows Heckmondwike Market Place. Near the fountain, erected in 1863, and its clock, added in 1904, stand single-deck tramcar number 62 and double-decker number 16. The former, showing destination Hightown, constituted part of a batch of six small cars, numbered 60 to 65, purchased in 1904. This location was also a starting point for horse-drawn carriages. *Postcard.*

On its way to Cleckheaton, the premier route of the YWD passed through Staincliffe, Heckmondwike and Liversedge. Hilly in places, it served well-populated industrial areas and was a potential money-spinner. On 7 April 1903, tramcar number 15 made a trial run from Staincliffe to Cleckheaton. As can be seen, it attracted a few inquisitive sightseers when it climbed past the market on Bradford Road, Cleckheaton. Its indicator suggests it had recently been running on the Thornhill route. The line was inspected by Major Druitt on 24 April 1903 and opened for passengers between Heckmondwike and Moorend the same day. The through service from Dewsbury to Moorend began on 29 July 1903. *Postcard.*

The extensive Flush Mills of T F Firth & Sons, manufacturers of woollen cloth, blankets and, eventually, carpets and rugs, are featured in this industrial tramscape at Westgate, Heckmondwike. Tramcar number 31 is on a trial run, possibly on 28 July 1903. Horses also must have passed by. *Postcard.*

With destination indicator showing Dewsbury, YWD tramcar number 39, in new condition, traverses Westgate, Heckmondwike, on its way towards the town's Market Place. *Postcard.*

During the 1914-18 War, tramway services were curtailed because of a shortage of coal (to produce power) and the call-up of employees into the forces. For the first time, the YWD employed women conductors (clippies). The following group of conductresses from Frost Hill depot trooped along to Alfred Henry Ramsden's studio in Wormald Street, Heckmondwike, for their group photograph. And smartly dressed they look! *Postcard.*

Another tramcar of the 7-48 batch, in this case number 36, proceeds along Station Road (part of Halifax Road), Millbridge, Liversedge, en route for Hightown, in about 1906. A decorative tram standard is nicely silhouetted against the sky. The premises of George Simpson & Son, tanners and curriers, are on the left. *Postcard: J Hodgson, photographer, Cleckheaton.*

Yorkshire Woollen tramcar number 42 pauses outside Littletown Post Office before returning to Dewsbury. In almost mint condition, it has Leather's Patent Ventilators above the windows and curtains inside them. Both these features were soon removed. The car seated twenty-two passengers inside on longitudinal slatted seats, and twenty-six outside on transverse wooden seats (later increased to thirty-four by replacing single with double seats). *Postcard.*

DEWSBURY
CHEMIST
WINCARNIS
BROOKE BONDS TEA
OVUM
NTMENT
48

Ready for its return to Dewsbury, tramcar number 28 rests beside Cleckheaton Town Hall on Bradford Road, thus allowing other travellers the freedom of the highway. The cart is probably laden with rags, for recycling into mungo or shoddy, to make heavy woollens. The tram itself shows an advert for a local newspaper. *Postcard.*

With destination indicator set at Dewsbury, tramcar number 27 has just passed Providence Place Congregational Chapel on Bradford Road at Cleckheaton. The year is 1904 and the newly erected telegraph poles have been painted white. *Postcard.*

Tram number 46, of the 7-48 batch, is pictured in its final form at Moorend terminus, Bradford Road, Cleckheaton, in about 1928. It has acquired high upper-deck side and balcony panels, giving a more modern appearance. *Postcard: Lilywhite number CKN 42.*

Tramway Employees' Sports Club

A substantial sum in aid of the Yorkshire (Woollen District) Electric Tramways Employees' Sports Club was raised by a whist drive and dance in Cleckheaton Town Hall last night. The club has as president Major Chapple, who is ably assisted by Mr H Gilbert, Cleckheaton, (secretary) and Mr A Ineson, Batley, (assistant secretary). The MCs for whist were Messrs H Bray (Dewsbury), N Rodgers (Batley), E Waite (Gomersal) and S Smith (Cleckheaton), and for dancing Messrs A Gill (Dewsbury) and J Roberts (Batley). The Tramways Orchestra played for dancing. Between 300 and 400 persons attended, and an enjoyable evening was spent by all.

Newspaper: *Batley News*, 30 April 1927.

In 1904, partly to reinforce the service on the Heckmondwike – Hightown route, the YWD purchased from Brush of Loughborough six small single-deck tramcars, numbered 60-65, with seating for twenty passengers. These cars were initially equipped with special regenerative controls to reduce power consumption. The Hightown spur, which continued up the Halifax Road from Liversedge, was largely composed of single track with passing loops. Here, at Hightown Heights terminus, the conductor and driver (the latter with his white summer cap attachment) pose with their pristine car, number 64. An unusual feature is the brake staff outside the dash. By 1924, two more large single-deck tramcars were required for the Ravensthorpe route. The bodies of four cars from the 60-65 batch were severed, then spliced together to form two seven-window cars. They were placed on new underframes and new trucks. The hybrid cars, with seating for thirty-six passengers, were numbered 55 and 61. (The original number 55 tramcar, a double-decker, came to grief in 1904 and, when repaired, exchanged numbers with single-deck car number 60). *Postcard: J Hodgson, Cleckheaton.*

A pair of YWD trams in their final form are seen passing each other on a steep and setted part of Halifax Road, Dewsbury, in the late 1920s. The old Dewsbury & District General Infirmary, with its Victorian tower, is on the right. *Postcard.*

The Market Place, Dewsbury, is featured with, at the far side, the Yorkshire Woollen tramway terminus. A tramcar of the 7-48 batch, in its final form, awaits departure, probably for Cleckheaton. The arch-fronted cinema, Public Benefit boot shop and Midland Bank (formerly London City & Midland) grace the background. J & B's (Johnson & Balmford's), locally famous drapers and milliners, is on the right. The old cab shelter is partly surrounded by taxis. *Postcard: B Matthews, photographer, Bradford, number 7659.*

Yorkshire Woollen District tramcar number 7 met with a fateful accident on 20 May 1904. The double-deck car had already been fitted with a top cover, and incorporated the usual hand brakes, Spencer 'Scotch' brake and Westinghouse magnetic slipper brake. A few days before the disaster, it had been in the repair shops having new wheels fitted. The work was completed on 18 May, when the car was taken out for a trial run by the shed foreman, who found it in good order. It was put back into service on 19 May, was in use all that day, and both drivers in charge reported it in good condition. On the day of the accident, it was taken out by driver Walter Stead of 8 Cliff Street, Dewsbury, who had been in the company's service for about fifteen months. Previously he had worked as a cab driver. After two or three weeks' training on the trams, he had driven them regularly. He had run them on the Cleckheaton-Dewsbury route without any problems.

Shortly before 3 o'clock on 20 May 1904, YWD tramcar number 7, driven by Walter Stead, was on a return trip from Cleckheaton to Dewsbury. Reaching the steep gradient near Dewsbury General Infirmary in Halifax Road, the driver applied his brakes, which failed to act. The car started to descend the hill at an alarming pace. Near the *Bath Hotel,* it knocked over a wagon of mineral waters driven by George Archer. At Willans Road, the tram driver was thrown off. Passengers attempting to leap off were restrained by the conductor, Arthur Oldroyd, of 8 Battye Street, Dewsbury, who stayed at his post. In Northgate, the runaway car crashed into the rear of a tram from Birkenshaw. The impact pitched the conductor of this tram, James George Harrison, through the plate glass window of Miss Fullerton's shop. A coal cart belonging to George Taylor was toppled on to the pavement, causing damage to the Bon Marche shop. A wagon owned by Gouthwaite Brothers, manufacturing chemists of Dewsbury Moor, was overturned, the bottles breaking and spilling vitriol on the road. The runaway car jumped off its own tracks and landed on the adjacent ones. Slowing down, it came to rest outside the London City & Midland Bank at the side of the Market Place, after lodging itself in a Ravensthorpe tram. Nobody was killed, but several people were injured, the severest cases being conveyed to Dewsbury Infirmary in cabs. A lady and gentleman on the perverse car, who were going to catch a train for Blackpool, were bruised, but refused to forego their Whitsuntide excursion. The damaged cars were taken to the depot at Savile Town, where number 7 is pictured. *Postcard*

At the Board of Trade enquiry, Major Druitt attributed blame to the driver rather than the brakes, and stated that a higher standard of training was needed.

The horse-drawn mineral water wagon, referred to above, belonged to Goldsborough & Sons of Thornhill Lees. The horse, a light bay gelding, was severely cut on the hocks, near-hind fetlock and withers. It was taken into the yard of the *Bath Hotel.* Force had to be used to induce it to return to Thornhill Lees. The driver of the wagon, George Archer, was interviewed by a representative of the *Dewsbury Reporter.* His story, which appeared in the 21 May edition, follows:

'I was coming up Victoria Road in order to get to the *Bath Hotel,* when a Dewsbury car ran past the top of the street. I was pleased at this, as I thought it would give me ten minutes for my business before another car came down. I drew up in front of the hotel and had only just reached the bar when there was a great crash. I rushed out and saw a shower of aerated water and broken glass descending on the road. My cart was smashed to atoms and the horse, stripped of all its gears, even the collar having been torn off, was being held by a bystander. In a second, the car was out of sight under the railway bridge. I had sixty dozen empties on my cart and thirty dozen full boxes. Only a dozen and a half were rescued. The horse was much cut. I am thankful I was not on the cart at the time, or I should not have been telling you this tale.'

An improved type of tramcar top cover was developed by William Rouse & Sons, the Heckmondwike coachbuilders, in 1908. It had five opening windows per side, those at each end being smaller than the central three. Canopies projected over the end balconies, and proper side panels (nicely painted and lined out) replaced the decency boards. In the above illustration, YWD tramcar number 25 has just emerged from the paint shop at Frost Hill depot, replete with its new top cover. The old balcony panels, with wire mesh above them, have been retained. This view clearly shows the reversed-type stairs, truck details and the BET magnet-and-wheel insignia on the waist panel. The headlamp shield may imply that the car was newly refurbished during or just after the 1914-18 War. However, the incorporation of window curtains is an enigma; perhaps they were a publicity gimmick for William Rouse or the BET. *Postcard.*

Many of the tramcars in the 7-48 batch received the improved type of top cover made by William Rouse & Sons from 1908 onwards. In postwar years, all trams of this batch were fitted with solid curved panels around each balcony in place of part solid and part mesh or rail surrounds. Tramcar number 23 therefore appears here in its final form around 1925 with the new maroon and primrose livery. The handbell, to warn unwary pedestrians and others, had replaced the foot gong of earlier days. Each car was provided with a single bell, which was transferred by the driver when he changed ends at the terminus. The latest Brush AA type truck is clearly visible. Well-known Dewsbury drapers and outfitters J&B (Johnson & Balmford) commandeered this tram for advertising, even extending it to the inside of the lower saloon. *Postcard.*

This illustration shows the opposite side and end of YWD tramcar number 23 to that on the previous page. The immaculate condition of the car and the smart advertising are worthy of note. *Photograph.*

If its Fashionable J&B's have it!
GET
-IN-
THIS CAR
AME
J&B's
MORLEY'S
HAVE YOU HEARD
DAMASCLI
FRISTER & ROSSMANN'S
SEWING MACHINES
B's.

Tramcar number 54 was part of the 49-56 batch of eight owned by Batley Corporation, but operated by the Yorkshire Woollen on the town's behalf. They were obtained from the British Electric Car Company, Trafford Park, Manchester, in 1903 and painted in Batley's own green livery. The 49-56 batch differed from the YWD's 7-48 batch in several ways. The waist band was slightly deeper and they had scrollwork around the upper deck (instead of wire mesh on the 7-48 batch). Lower-deck seating was cane rattan instead of wooden slats. After 1908, the Batley cars were given top covers, with five windows per side and extended canopies, similar to those used on the YWD cars. The scrollwork on the balconies was retained. The cars owned by Batley Corporation were primarily intended for use on the former Bradford Road steam route; however, they were used on other Batley-centred routes, as the above photograph testifies. Tramcar number 54 is seen passing the *George Inn* on High Street as it nears Heckmondwike, having commenced its journey at Batley Market Place. *Postcard.*

Batley Corporation tramcar number 60 stands at the terminus in Batley Market Place, before leaving for Heckmondwike via Healey Lane, about 1906. The Town Hall is on the right. Tramcar number 60 was formerly number 55, but after the accidents shown on pages 48 and 49, exchanged numbers with single-deck car number 60. *Postcard.*

An unidentified YWD tramcar of the 7-48 batch rests on Commercial Street, at Batley Market Place terminus, before departing for Hecknondwike via Healey Lane. About half the batch had not received top covers by 1907 – this is one of them. The imposing building to the left is the Batley Co-operative Society's new central premises, opened in 1906, but now demolished. Also visible near the tram is the Maypole shop, of tea and butter fame. *Postcard: Ernest R Slater, 1 Basinghall Square, Leeds.*

DEIGHTON-BATLEY
MILLINERY, MANTLES, FURS
DRESSES, CARPETS, CURTAINS
55
55

Left: On 16 January 1904, Batley Corporation tramcar number 55 ran out of control when descending Thorncliffe Road towards Track Road. As shown, it crashed through a boundary wall at Hyrstlands House, the home of Dewsbury textile manufacturer and former MP, Mr Mark Oldroyd. Nobody was killed but three people were injured. At the official enquiry, blame was attached to the driver, who probably approached the corner too fast and failed to apply the brakes correctly. *Postcard.*

On 29 August 1904, Batley tramcar number 55, back in service after repairs, had a further mishap when rounding a corner near the *New Inn* in Purlwell Lane. The car, having got out of control, ran into a horse-drawn van belonging to George Parrott, a confectioner of Commercial Street, Batley. Its driver was delivering pastries to Mr Driffield's eating house on the right of the picture. Nobody was badly injured. The rebellious tramcar was again repaired. On grounds of superstition, its number was changed to 60. *Postcard.*

Amphibious trams, nearly! Until recent times, the lower levels of Batley and Dewsbury were prone to flooding from their respective becks. This photograph, from 25 May 1925, shows Yorkshire Woollen and Batley Corporation tramcars on Bradford Road, Batley Carr. Nearest the camera is an unnumbered YWD tram from the 7-48 batch, in almost final form, with top cover and solid panels around the balconies. Behind it is Batley Corporation tram number 51, also in near final form. The single-deck car is part of a YWD batch numbered 70-81. These were purchased second-hand from Sheffield Corporation in 1919-20, having originated with that municipality twenty years earlier. These cars had five windows per side, and seated 28 passengers inside, but the YWD added two seats on each platform behind the driving position. At the end of the line (actually in front) is YWD tram number 8. *Postcard: Mark Cross, photographer, Borough Studio, 40 Market Place, Dewsbury.*

Tram standards and single track are seen disappearing into the distance up a steep part of Purlwell Lane at Batley. Purlwell Council School, dating from 1874, is behind the trees on the right. *Postcard.*

The Junction at Heckmondwike is shown in about 1910. Here, High Street (left) ends; the road diverges into Batley Road (centre) and Halifax Road (right, off the picture). Tramcar number 55 climbs into Batley Road on its way to Batley Market Place. This car had been number 60, but exchanged numbers with the original number 55, a double-decker, after the latter was involved in a pair of accidents (featured on pages 48 and 49). On the left is one of the many Lion grocery and provision stores in the area. *Postcard: J Hodgson, Cleckheaton.*

A Batley Corporation tramcar of the 49-56 batch descends steep Batley Road, past the *Craven Heifer*, as it heads towards High Street, Heckmondwike in about 1906. The roof of Healey Council School is visible in the distance over the trees. *Postcard.*

Further up Batley Road, the highway becomes Healey Lane and passes Healey Council School, shown towards the right of this picture. The carriage (with Dr and Mrs Erskine Stuart) is standing at the corner with White Lea Road. At the opposite side (on the right), tram track, laid by Batley Corporation, can be seen curving into Common Road (and actually running along most of its length). The intention to carry this through to Halifax Road, which, more or less would have completed a circular route for Batley's trams, never materialized, the YWD regarding it as superfluous. The junction was constructed at the convergence of Halifax Road with Batley Road/High Street, without a direct turn from Batley Road into Halifax Road. *Postcard.*

Road works, in connection with track laying, still seem to be in hand on Oxford Road, Great Gomersal (near the Gomersal Co-op shop on the right), probably in late September or early October 1903. This is part of the Liversedge (*Swan Inn*), Gomersal and Birkenshaw section of the YWD system, opened for public service on 13 October. Tramcar number 41 is on a trial run. *Postcard.*

This is another 'first' tram through Gomersal, actually number 44 on 2 October 1903. Excited children from Hilltop National School, left, line the footpath. Concern had been expressed at the closeness of the tram lines to the school. The official inspection of the route took place on 13 October, and the trams started picking up passengers immediately afterwards. Through cars were run from Dewsbury to Birkenshaw, via Gomersal. *Postcard.*

Driver Sam Cooper holds the controls of YWD tramcar number 19 at Birkenshaw terminus, prior to the return journey to Dewsbury. Observe the 'fresh air' passenger seat on the balcony. *Postcard.*

YWD tramcar number 8 is pictured on a return journey from Birkenshaw to Dewsbury, via the old steam tram route through Birstall and Batley. In the background is Brookroyd Post Office, midway between Birstall and Batley. It must be summer; the car windows are open and the driver and conductor are not too muffled up. The open driving platforms were said to be good for drivers with lung problems! Two different types of top cover are clearly illustrated on this page, the one on tramcar number 19 being a later version with thicker wooden strips above the windows for extra strength. *Postcard.*

A policeman stands between the setted tram tracks at Birstall Smithies, about 1930, on the old steam tram route which was converted to electric in 1905. The *Railway Hotel* in the centre and 'open day and night' garage on the right call to mind the competition. *Postcard: Lilywhite, number BAL 2.*

This is one of two tramcars of the 7-48 batch which were modified to fit under the low railway bridges on the Ravensthorpe route. The trolley standards and destination boxes were lowered. The Board of Trade refused permission to run them because of danger to passengers. One of the tramcars, shown below and possibly number 9, was decorated with coloured lights and bunting for the Dewsbury Amalgamaton celebrations of 1910. The population of the new Borough of Dewsbury increased from 28,000 to 53,000, with the incorporation of Ravensthorpe, Thornhill, Earlsheaton and part of Soothill Upper. A further accolade came in 1913 when the County Borough of Dewsbury was created. *Postcard.*

The creator of this photograph didn't have far to walk! The Borough Studio of Mark Cross, 40 Market Place, Dewsbury, is behind the tramcar. To the left, at 44 Market Place, is Broadhead's linen warehouse. The tram is one of the spliced cars, either number 55 or 61, mentioned on page 38. The decorations are in celebration of Dewsbury's Shopping Week in September 1925. The car toured the area and was illuminated after dark. *Postcard: Mark Cross, Dewsbury.*

Here, tramcar number 55 or 61 is decorated for one of the Batley Festivals, using some of the same bunting and fairy lights as in the top photograph. The driver's handbell is visible on both these shots. *Postcard.*

Front view! Tramcars normally had no front or rear; only two ends. After reaching a terminus, the driving end became the back end and vice versa. The driver walked to the opposite end, taking the control key, and possibly a sand pedal and handbell with him. Meanwhile, the conductor swivelled the trolley boom, perhaps with the aid of a bamboo pole. Passengers might have found that the upper-deck seats needed turning to face the direction of travel. People boarded and alighted at the back end, this usually being the conductor's domain when not collecting money and issuing tickets in the saloon or upstairs. The photographer paid more attention to the humans than the tram when he composed this picture. Their identity is unknown, but some, at least, probably worked as YWD maintenance staff. Was it a family get-together? The tramcar must be either number 19, 29 or 39 (probably 29). It had likely been fitted with a top cover; certainly the foot-gong had been replaced with a handbell. Joseph Wilson was a tailor at 17 Corporation Street, Dewsbury. *Postcard.*

Following the difficulties brought about by the 1914-18 War, some restoration of the YWD tramcar fleet took place. But by the late 1920s, worn track, impending running out of leases, and improvements in motorbuses led to talk of tramway abandonments. With the passing of a Yorkshire (Woollen District) Transport Bill in 1931, the way was open for the withdrawal of the trams. The routes were closed down in stages. First to go, on 19 March 1932, were the Liversedge – Hightown and Birstall and Birkenshaw sections. Last in line was the Dewsbury – Cleckheaton section, which closed on Wednesday 31 October 1934. People turned out along the route to wave goodbye to the two last trams. The one for the public left Dewsbury at 11.20 pm. The other, for officials and representatives of local authorities, departed at 11.30 pm. The last public car was driven by Mr Jack Armitage of Mount Pleasant, Batley, who had Mr J Ashton of Thornhill Lees as conductor. The officials' car, number 11, was in charge of Mr Arthur Hanson, a foreman, whilst Chief Inspector Gardner acted as conductor, although fares were not collected. The Mayor of Dewsbury, Councillor H F Shaw, was at the controls. At the Batley border, near the *Shoulder of Mutton*, the Mayor of Batley, Councillor G Elsie Taylor, took over the controls. At the *Junction Inn*, Councillor T W Crowther, chairman of Heckmondwike District Council, took the controls, to cries of 'Are ta gettin' t'steam up, Tom?' Beyond Heckmondwike Market Place, Councillor Andrew Stott JP, vice-chairman of Spenborough District Council, took command and the journey was continued to Frost Hill, where an audience of local residents had gathered. Employees of the company greeted the approach of the last tram with a 'peal', sounded on bells obtained from the available trams in the depot. The illustrations, from the *Dewsbury Reporter*, show the last tram, number 11, leaving Dewsbury Market Place with the Mayor of Dewsbury and, secondly, the Mayor of Batley in control at the Dewsbury-Batley boundary.

CHAPTER 3

Yorkshire (West Riding) Electric Tramways Co Ltd

The history of Wakefield owes much to the bridge over the River Calder, which provided a link to the south. The town became famous for its cattle and corn markets. Coal mining, textiles and engineering were determinants in its growth. It was advantaged by the coming of the canals – the Aire & Calder, the Calder & Hebble and the Barnsley. The railways brought competition for the canals, in the transporting of raw materials and finished products. Their variable success as passenger carriers was overshadowed by the coming of the trams. Paradoxically, the River Calder, or more correctly the bridge over it, was cited as a deterrent to their introduction.

By the granting of a charter in 1888, Wakefield was made a city. It became the administrative centre of the West Riding of Yorkshire. It still occupies an important position as head of the Wakefield Metropolitan District, which includes Castleford, Pontefract, Normanton, Ossett and Horbury, plus the districts around Sandal and Outwood. These are the areas which were served by the Wakefield-based tramway company. The route north from Wakefield actually reached the City of Leeds. Perversely, the Normanton-Castleford-Pontefract section was never linked to the Wakefield-centred routes.

The first reference to a tramway for Wakefield goes back to 1862. Twenty years later, a proposal was put forward to run cable or steam trams from St Michael's Church in Westgate, through Wakefield, over Chantry Bridge and on to Sandal and Agbrigg. (The 'new' bridge over the Calder was not opened until 1933). Owners of some of the properties on Little Westgate, along which the trams would have run, objected. The Justices of the Peace, who were responsible for maintenance of Chantry Bridge, were worried about the trams damaging or even falling through the structure.

In 1901, after several rival groups had announced plans for electric trams in and around Wakefield, a survey was made of existing traffic over Chantry Bridge. It was taken between Wednesday 1 May and Saturday 4 May inclusive. In both directions, on the four days, totals of 5,304 horse-drawn vehicles, 8 traction engines, 15 motorcars, 3,530 bicycles and 629 horses and cattle traversed the bridge. Individual statistics for each day were fairly even, with two exceptions. On Wednesday, 423 horses and cattle were recorded, due to the livestock market. On Saturday, 1,740 bicycles were recorded. On that same day, in a forty-five minute period, 25,000 people walked over the bridge. They were going to the rugby ground at Belle Vue. It was, of course, pointed out that if trams were used, the number of walkers and cyclists would be lower. However, the West Riding County Council, which had become responsible for the bridge, was definitely not in favour of widening it.

Of the various syndicates formed to operate tramways in the Wakefield area, the Wakefield & District Light Railway Company was the successful contender. Colonel Von Donop inspected Chantry Bridge in June 1901 and, in spite of reservations, recommended to the Board of Trade that authorisation to build an electric tramway be given. Through the *Light Railway Orders* granted in 1901 and 1902, the company was empowered to construct lines from Wakefield to Agbrigg, Sandal, Ossett and the Leeds boundary, plus a branch from Rothwell Haigh to Rothwell. In 1905, the Wakefield company was acquired by the newly registered Yorkshire (West Riding) Electric Tramways Company, which had already obtained authorisation to build tramways in the Castleford, Normanton and Pontefract areas. This company had been registered in April 1905 to operate a network of fifty route miles of tramways in the West Riding. Only half of these were ever constructed. The name was perpetuated, however, with the Wakefield and Castleford centred lines. The 'West Riding' label only disappeared from the succeeding buses after the 'Arriva' takeover.

The main contractor for the tramways was Dick, Kerr & Company of Preston. The through line from Sandal to Thwaite Gate was mainly double track, although the section from Sandal to the Wakefield outskirts was single track with passing loops until 1925. From Robin Hood to Stourton, at the edge of Leeds, the tramway passed through sparsely populated agricultural country, noted for its rhubarb. The spur to Rothwell was largely single track with passing loops. The through line from Agbrigg to Ossett was largely double track, apart from a section along Station Road at Ossett which was single with passing loops. A stretch of single track along part of Doncaster Road was doubled in 1925.

The principal depot was erected at Belle Isle, a good mile south of the centre of Wakefield, on the site of a former dyeworks. The property backed on to the River Calder. Coal for the generating plant was brought in barges and unloaded at a wharf. Water for the boilers and the condensing plant was taken from the river. Two smaller depots, with substations, were erected at Rothwell Haigh and Sowood, Ossett.

By August 1904, all the lines except those on the Rothwell branch were ready for the Board of Trade inspection. This was carried out on 9 August 1904 by Major Druitt and other officials who toured the system. Subject to some speed restrictions being introduced and a few minor alterations being made, the lines were passed for public use. The official opening day was Monday 15 August 1904 and, according to local reports, everyone seemed to enjoy themselves. There was no timekeeping and some of the cars ran in convoy.

Meanwhile, construction of the branch from Rothwell Haigh to Rothwell continued. This was opened to the public in December 1904, the trams terminating at Thwaite Gate, as did those from Wakefield. The incovenience of having to transfer from a Wakefield company car to a Leeds City car in order to reach the centre of Leeds was alleviated from 1 June 1905 onwards. The Wakefield trams commenced running to a terminal loop near Kirkgate Market, Corn Exchange, Leeds. By a reciprocal agreement, Leeds Corporation trams took over the Rothwell service and used the same terminus loop in Leeds.

When construction of the Wakefield tramways was nearing completion, work on the Normanton, Castleford and Pontefract lines was about to begin. In Castleford's Aire Street and Carlton Street, digging operations were halted by cash and other disputes, causing much annoyance to shopkeepers. When completed, the tracks in Castleford remained unused for several months because those in Normanton and Pontefract had not been put out to tender. Dick, Kerr & Company became the main contractors. The Castleford Depot was built in Wheldon Lane, with the company's own power station adjacent.

The first trial run, carrying various officials over the Castleford and Normanton section, took place on 9 October 1906. Three days later, a similar run was made over the whole system. The Board of Trade inspection was carried out on 20 October by Major J W Pringle, who then announced that operating powers would be granted. On Thursday, 25 October, the formal opening took place. Guests were carried over the system in specially decorated cars, to the acclaim of adults and children, who lined the streets or tried to follow the trams. The tramway was opened to the public on Monday, 29 October 1906.

The Yorkshire (West Riding) Electric Tramways Company operated a fleet of double-deck tramcars. Those which started life with open upper decks were later top covered. The comprehensive contracts which were worked out with the Dick, Kerr Company included the supply of tramcars from their Preston works. However, eight second-hand trams with Brush bodies were hired, then purchased, from Leeds Corporation in 1917-19 to replace cars destroyed in a fire at Castleford Depot in March 1917.

The original livery of the West Riding tramcars was principally crimson lake and cream. The initials of the Wakefield & District Light Railway Company were carried on a garter design on the waist panels. Due to shortage of paint during the 1914-18 War, the livery was changed to two shades of green. Later, some of the cars were painted battleship grey. Other colours were used, depending on availability of paint. From this period, the garter bore the full title of Yorkshire (West Riding) Electric Tramways Company Limited. From 1924 onwards, a new livery was devised by Robert England, company secretary, who was the son of the then managing director, Harry England. A brighter shade of green, with cream, was introduced. An impressive new emblem, which comprised the White Rose of Yorkshire between the words 'West' and 'Riding', was featured on each waist panel.

The total route mileage on the full West Riding tramway system was almost twenty-five miles. By 1906, the fleet consisted of sixty-seven tramcars and remained so for many years. Proposed extensions from Wakefield to Ardsley and Alverthorpe never materialized, nor did connections from Rothwell to Castleford (via Methley), Wakefield to Normanton (via Stanley) or Wakefield to Pontefract (via Featherstone). The flagship route was from Sandal to Leeds, via Wakefield. To encourage usage even further, the company opened a pleasure and amusement park at Lofthouse in 1908. The route to Ossett greatly benefitted the residents of Horbury, whose railway station was down a long steep hill. Uniquely for its size, Ossett later became host to two tramway companies.

The 1914-18 War caused a number of problems; these were compacted by a disastrous fire at Castleford Depot on 5 March 1917, when eight cars were destroyed. The track on the Normanton-Castleford-Pontefract section was bedevilled by mining subsidence. Several omnibus concerns in the area countered with bus competition. In most years, it was claimed that the Castleford trams ran at a loss and were subsidised by the Wakefield trams, which carried four-fifths of the company's passengers.

There were few surprises when the West Riding company announced that the last tramcars in the Castleford area would run on Sunday 1 November 1925, and be replaced by the company's buses. In the event, no special ceremony was held. Under the *Road Traffic Act* of 1930, railway companies were allowed to buy an interest in existing bus companies. The WR company managed to remain independent. Nevertheless, having become a sizeable bus operator, it decided to abandon the remainder of its tramways. The final day of operation on the Leeds-Sandal and Leeds-Rothwell routes was Tuesday, 31 May 1932. The last cars to Ossett and Agbrigg ran on Monday, 25 July 1932.

Although the Yorkshire (West Riding) Electric Tramways never reached the full potential, the company was in many ways a pioneer. The tramcars on the Wakefield routes were replaced by a fleet of new double-deck centre-entrance Leyland Titans, with attractive bodywork by Charles H Roe of Cross Gates. These bright red buses (all the other WR buses were green) proved to be worthy successors to the trams.

The principal depot for the Yorkshire (West Riding) Electric Tramways Company was built at Belle Isle, off Barnsley Road, Wakefield. The company's generating station and repair and paint shops were erected alongside. All of them were on the site of the former Holdsworth's Belle Isle Dyeworks, which backed on to the River Calder. These dyeworks had become redundant when increasing numbers of textile firms set up their own dyeing procedures. The work of building the tramway depot and ancillary structures (and demolishing old buildings) commenced in early 1904. The steam raising plant consisted of four Lancashire Boilers, manufactured by Spurr, Inman & Company of nearby Calder Vale Road. Much of the water needed for the boilers was drawn from the Calder. A fuel economiser was supplied by E Green & Son, also of Calder Vale Road. Most of the electrical equipment was made by Dick, Kerr, who were specialists in the field. A series of photographs was taken by Edwin I Walker, photographer, of 28 Wood Street, Wakefield, featuring stages in construction of Belle Isle Depot. Most of them show a date. The one below, although not dated, was probably taken in February 1904. Barnsley Road is visible in the background. Clearly, a lot of excavation work has taken place on the right and in the foreground, the latter for the laying of five sets of tracks with inspection pits. *Postcard: E I Walker, photographer, Wood Street, Wakefield.*

The construction of part of the Belle Isle Depot complex, in early 1904, is shown on this similar photograph to the previous one, but with the camera moved slightly to the left. *Postcard: E I Walker, Wakefield.*

Looking in the opposite direction to the two previous shots, this view, dated 30 March 1904, shows work in progress on the main car shed, whose partially built walls are visible on the left and in the background. Two of the inspection pits have been dug. A couple of dozen men, picks and shovels at the ready, still have the task of moving much of the earth on the right. *Postcard: E I Walker, Wakefield.*

This photograph, from 28 April 1904, shows progress to the car shed. The inspection pits are developing and the walls are gaining height. *Postcard: E I Walker, Wakefield.*

On a photograph, dated 30 March 1904, the new generating station at Belle Isle is pictured under construction. Some old riverside buildings are visible in the background. *Postcard: E I Walker, Wakefield.*

The same structure looks to be almost complete on this photograph taken on 12 April from the opposite end. The stylish twin buildings, in brick, have clerestory roofs. Spouting has been rigged up to convey water from the guttering to a storage tank. *Postcard: E I Walker, Wakefield.*

The generating station is featured on this undated view, taken across the River Calder. Four boilers are just visible inside the nearest building. *Postcard: E I Walker, Wakefield.*

Inside the same building, four Lancashire Boilers are in place. *Postcard: E I Walker, Wakefield.*

By 30 April, the date of this photograph, these two generators, of Dick, Kerr manufacture, had been installed. *Postcard: E I Walker, Wakefield.*

One of four boilers, supplied to the Wakefield & District Light Railway Company by Spurr, Inman & Company, is displayed outside their Calder Vale Road works, prior to its short journey to Belle Isle. Spurr, Inman was established in 1863 for the making of Lancashire and Cornish Boilers. *Photograph.*

Whilst the depot and generating plant were being built at Belle Isle, the installation of track, cables, poles and wiring was proceeding apace in various parts of Wakefield and the surrounding areas. Here, on Chantry Bridge, three men are precariously perched on top of one of the Dick, Kerr tower wagons, as they assemble overhead wiring. The forbidding looking buildings are part of King's Mill. This was eventually demolished to make way for a less-circuitous bridge, which carried the replacement buses when the tramway closed. *Postcard: E I Walker, Wakefield.*

Workmen, having excavated part of the road known as Westgate in Wakefield, are laying track on a bed of concrete, which they have mixed on a wooden platform. Dimly visible on the left is the Theatre Royal; on the right is the *Albion Hotel*. Some lads on the left seem more interested in watching the workers than delivering newspapers. *Postcard: E I Walker, Wakefield.*

Slightly further up Westgate, similar work is in progress, probably in April 1904. The granite setts at the side of the road will shortly be fitted between and on each side of the rails. In the background is the Yorkshire Penny Bank, since rebuilt (with a slight change of name). The 'audience' includes many children. *Postcard: E I Walker, Wakefield.*

HALDANE
AND
ELLIOTT.
RE
ANK.
WATSON & KENWORTHY

By the early 1900s, Wakefield's Bull Ring, or Market Place, was a highly developed shopping and socialising area. With its convergence of roads, it appropriately became the tramway centre. Here, in early 1904, workmen are shown laying a labyrinth of tram lines in the Bull Ring. These consist of $6\frac{1}{2}''$ deep girder sections, with $1\frac{1}{2}''$ deep grooves for the tram wheels, much rivetting being involved. The piled-up granite setts, removed so that work can proceed, will eventually be repositioned. A lady in an upstairs room of the *Griffin Hotel*, to the left of the Maypole shop, has a grandstand view. *Postcard: E I Walker, Wakefield.*

Cables are being laid on the east side of Leeds Road, between Outwood and Lofthouse Gate. Side poles with bracket arms are in place, but not track. The three-core lead-covered cables ran from the generating station at Belle Isle to a sub-station at Rothwell Haigh. *Postcard: E I Walker, Wakefield.*

In October 1903, the Wakefield & District Light Railway Company ordered fifty-five tramcars from Dick, Kerr & Company of Preston. The order stipulated delivery of thirty of them by the middle of 1904. The first eighteen cars were delivered by the Lancashire & Yorkshire Railway Company to the goods yard at Kirkgate Station, Wakefield. The illustrations on this page show the first two cars to arrive, numbers 5 and 12, on 25 June 1904. The windows of each tramcar carry advertising blurbs for the Electric Railway & Tramway Carriage Works, Preston. This was a subsiduary of Dick, Kerr. Temporary track was laid along Park Street so that the cars could be moved on to permanent track in Kirkgate. From there they were pulled to Belle Isle Depot where upper decks were fitted. *Postcards: E I Walker, Wakefield.*

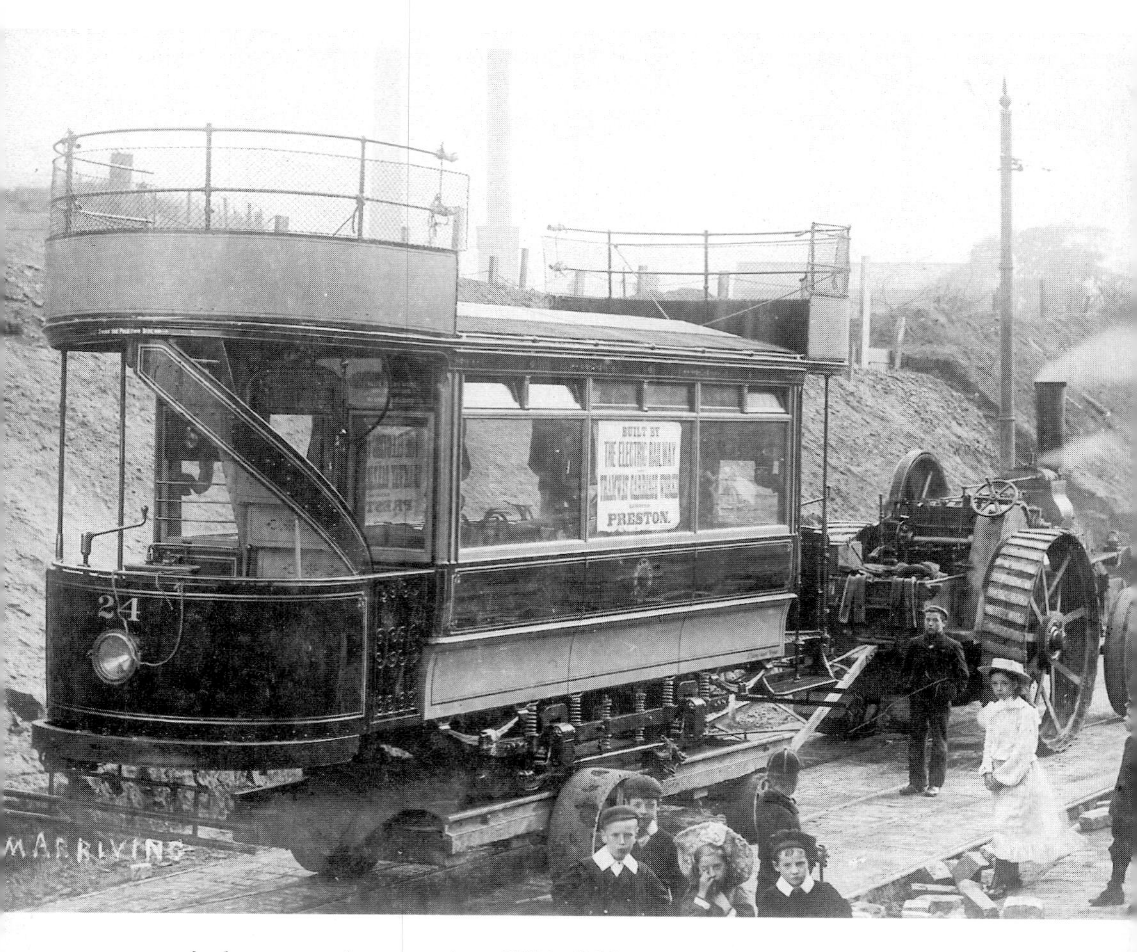

At least two pictures exist of Wakefield tramcars being delivered on low loaders by traction engine in 1904. This photograph of car number 24 was taken just inside the depot yard at Belle Isle. The upper deck of the tram is incomplete, although the balcony ends have been fitted. It can perhaps be assumed that not all the tramcars arrived at Belle Isle by the same method. In small lettering at the end of the car, under the balcony, are the words, 'Swing the pole this side', with an arrow pointing to the right. *Postcard: E I Walker, Wakefield.*

Tramcar number 12, of the 1-30 batch, is also seen inside the depot yard at Belle Isle, on a card which carries the caption, 'The first car run through Wakefield.' The car, in finished condition, already carries advertisements for several local firms, including Ralph Bell and their acclaimed table waters. These tramcars seated twenty-two passengers inside on longitudinal seats, and thirty-four outside on transverse seats. Six electric lights brightened the lower deck. The two 'oyster' lights on the upper deck can be seen. The curtains were a short-lived feature. *Postcard: E I Walker, Wakefield.*

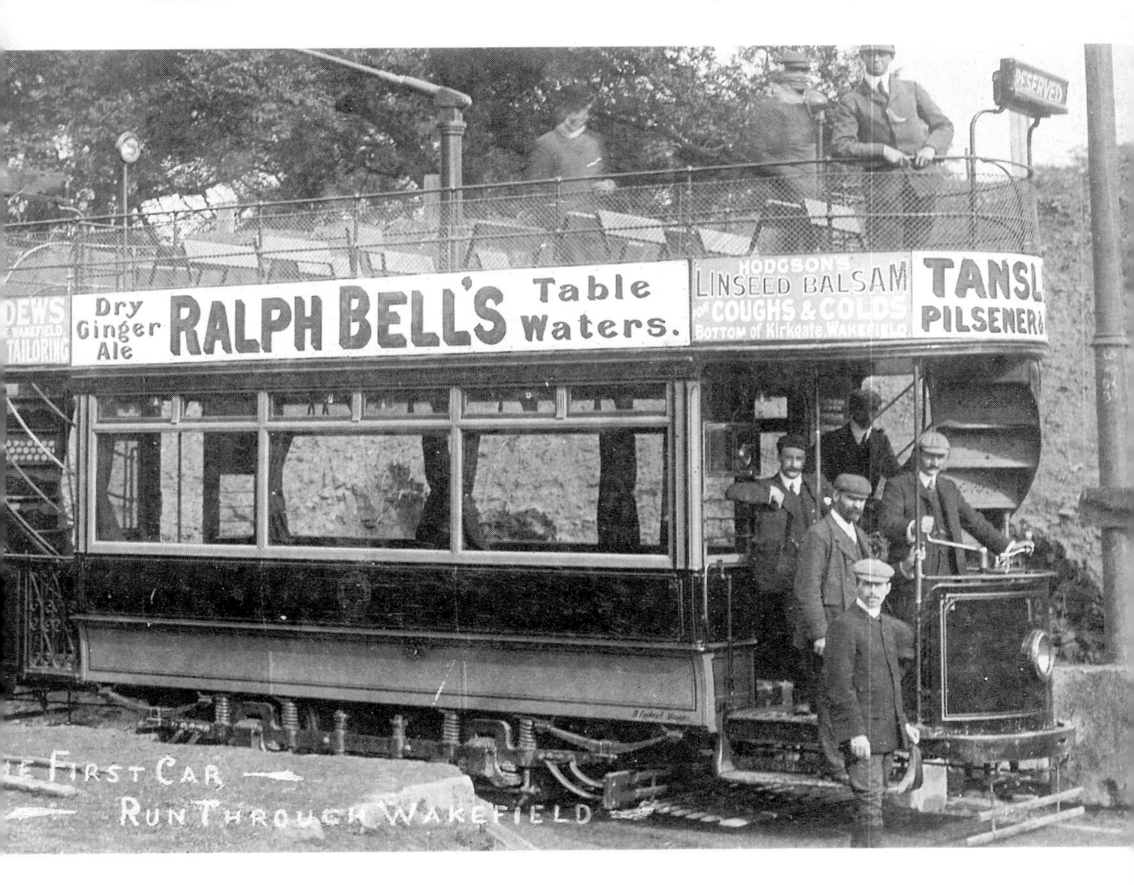

This view inside the depot yard, with Barnsley Road in the distance on the right, features tramcar number 23, probably in August 1904. Several adverts for local concerns adorn the vehicle, and the angle of photography gives a good view of the reversed type stairway. *Postcard: George & John Hall, Cathedral Studio, Little Westgate, Wakefield.*

West Riding tramcar number 10 makes a pre-opening trial run along Doncaster Road, Belle Vue, near Agbrigg, in July 1904. Its destination indicator is a slight exaggeration! *Postcard.*

The first tramcar through Wakefield, on 22 July 1904, was number 13. With the heads of a few pedestrians turned, it is seen climbing Upper Kirkgate, its destination indicator set at Castleford. The route from Wakefield to Castleford was never constructed. The buildings on the left have survived to the present day, but those on the right were demolished in the 1950s for road widening. They include the *Bull & Mouth Hotel*, Home & Colonial Stores and Slaters of tea and coffee fame. *Postcard: E I Walker, Wakefield.*

The crowds in the Bull Ring, Wakefield, indicate that this is the day of the public opening of the tramway, 15 August 1904. The tram in the centre is about to begin its journey up the Leeds Road; that on the right carries a destination blind set at Ossett. This photograph makes an interesting comparison with that at the top of page 74. *Postcard: G & J Hall, Wakefield.*

By the middle of 1905, the probable date of this photograph, tramcars were providing a regular service between Sandal and Leeds. Here, in the Bull Ring, car number 5 awaits departure for Leeds, whilst number 15 emerges from Northgate, having journeyed from Leeds. The *Griffin Hotel* is on the right. On weekdays, the service operated from around 5 o'clock in the morning until after midnight. *Postcard: Phototype Company, Ventnor Street, Leeds.*

The tramway passenger service from Agbrigg to Ossett, via Wakefield and Horbury, was launched on 15 August 1904. The inaugural West Riding tram, number 16, is captured emerging from the end of Station Road into Ossett's Bank Street. *Postcard.*

Two of the first West Riding tramcars, having arrived in Ossett from Wakefield on 15 August 1904, stand at the terminus in Bank Street. They are well-filled with passengers for the return journey to Wakefield and Agbrigg. Part of the Pickard Memorial Fountain is visible on the left. The terminus was moved nearer to Ossett Town Hall in 1908, to share a common loop with trams from Dewsbury, which are dealt with later. *Postcard.*

This and the next few pages trace the West Riding tramway route from Sandal to Leeds. The above picture shows the terminus outside the *Castle Inn* at Sandal, looking towards Wakefield, in 1904, when the cars only ran as far as Thwaite Gate. *Postcard.*

The message on the reverse of this card, postmarked 25 October 1904, reads, ‘The car is half way down the village. They are going splendid now.’ But, according to the indicator, still only as far as Thwaite Gate. The tramcar is standing just short of the Sandal terminus and facing Wakefield. *Postcard: G & J Hall, Wakefield.*

West Riding tramcar number 47, depicted here at Sandal terminus in about 1908, was part of the second batch of cars, numbers 31 to 55. Delivered in 1905, they also came from the Electric Railway & Tramway Carriage Works at Preston, but with top covers incorporated. The cars had four windows per side downstairs instead of three, the extra stanchions providing greater support for the upper decks. In 1924, an off-road terminus with passenger shelter was constructed a short distance south of the *Castle Inn* on the east side of Barnsley Road. This survived as a bus terminus after cessation of tramway operation. *Postcard.*

WR tramcar number 2 heads away from the camera along Barnsley Road towards Wakefield in the Haddingley Hill area of Sandal, around 1910. The track hereabouts was single, with passing loops, until 1925, when double track was laid. On the extreme right is the *Forester's Arms* with, beyond it, Providence Terrace. *Postcard: Phototype Company, Leeds.*

LEEDS
R.P. GREEN.
TAILOR & COSTUMIER
16 UPPER KIRKGATE WAKEFIELD
Hill Sandal

Taken in about 1905, this photograph shows a now radically altered part of Wakefield known as Bridge End. Tram tracks for Agbrigg and Sandal diverge into Doncaster Road, left, and Barnsley Road, right. The *White Bear,* centre, and most of the other properties shown have been demolished. *Postcard: G & J Hall, Wakefield.*

'S TADCASTER ALES

A tramcar of the 1-30 batch crosses Chantry Bridge, Wakefield, in 1905, on its way to Sandal (or Agbrigg). Beyond the Chantry Chapel of St Mary can be seen part of one of the city's industrial complexes. *Postcard.*

A pair of tramcars, from the first and second batches delivered to the WR, rub shoulders at the lower end of Wakefield's Kirkgate. The building on the left is the now-demolished *Crown Hotel;* in the background is the bridge carrying the railway into Kirkgate Station. The tramcar on the left, number 33, is destined for Thwaite Gate; this dates the picture to the first part of 1905. The car on the right, number 9, is bound for Agbrigg. *Postcard: G & J Hall, Wakefield.*

Tramcar number 46 descends Upper Kirkgate on its way to Sandal, in the days when the Lipton shop at the end of Teall Street sold tea and other commodities and Wakefield Cathedral was surrounded by iron railings. *Postcard.*

Tramcar number 4 stands in the Market Place (Bull Ring), Wakefield, awaiting departure for Leeds, a few years after the monument of Queen Victoria was unveiled in 1905. In the foreground, the various sets of tracks merge into one, to facilitate passage up a rather narrow Northgate. *Postcard: Raphael Tuck & Sons, London.*

Northwards from Wakefield, the West Riding tramway passed through a group of developing residential areas, including Newton Hill, Outwood, Lofthouse and Robin Hood. A lot of employment was found in local collieries and nearby mills. By 1910, the road through Newton Hill and Outwood was characterized by terraces of brick houses, most of them still in existence. The coming of the trams meant that these were ideal areas in which to live. This view from around 1907 shows the part of Newton Hill leading up to Red Hall Lane. The pole on the right has a couple of span wires to help keep the main wires to the curvature of the road. *Postcard.*

Tramcar number 39 ascends Leeds Road at Outwood, on its way to Leeds, seven miles away. The children, posing for the photographer, seem to be in no danger from other traffic. The *Queen Hotel* is on the left. *Postcard: A & G Taylor, photographers, 84 Manningham Lane, Bradford.*

Tram number 1, en route for Sandal, is about to pass Bright Eyes Row, Lofthouse, shown on the left in late 1904. Many of the houses in the area were occupied by workers at Robin Hood's collieries, by-product plant or quarries. *Postcard: James Wilberforce Ineson, printer & stationer, Rothwell.*

A cyclist obscures the fleet number of a tramcar of the 68-75 batch, purchased from Leeds in 1919, and shown passing schools on either side of the road, as it descends towards the *Half Way House* at Robin Hood in the early 1920s. The nearby Robin Hood Station had opened on 4 January 1904, but was closed to passengers on 1 October 1904, due, it was claimed, to tramcar competition. *Postcard.*

With Bell Hill falling away in th distance, WR tramcar number 25 creates a sligh stir as it pauses o the main Wakefield-Leeds Road at the junction with Wood Lane, in August 1904. Rothwell Haigh Depot had been built on land just off the picture to the right. *Postcard.*

The Rothwell branch ran along Wood Lane, Ingram Parade and Maxwell Street, and terminated on Commercial Street, Rothwell. From 1 June 1905, it was served almost exclusively by cars of Leeds City Tramways. However, this view along Commercial Street shows the West Riding works car, probably on maintenance duty. *Postcard: William Bramley, the Electric Printing Works, Cross Gates, Leeds.*

Having just left its terminus on a roundabout at the top of Kirkgate (near Leeds Market), a WR tramcar makes its way along Duncan Street, with the Corn Exchange in the background, before turning into Lower Briggate, on its journey back to Sandal. The destination indicator shows 'Wakefield'; it was customary to change this to 'Sandal' before reaching Outwood. *Postcard: J Valentine & Sons, Dundee.*

Leeds City tramcar number 64 stands at the terminus near the *Black Bull* (Tetley's Fine Ales) in Rothwell, before returning to the Corn Exchange, Leeds. The car, photographed here in about 1910, was introduced, complete with top cover, in 1904. The route, from Rothwell to Thwaite Gate, had been operated by West Riding trams for only a short period. *Postcard.*

When a Miner is Not a Workman

The Wakefield & District Light Railway Company, on Monday, at Wakefield, summoned a miner named James Kershaw, residing at Wakefield, on two charges of refusing to pay tram fares. It was stated that on the 15th September the defendant rode on a tramcar from Wakefield to Outwood, and only paid a penny instead of twopence, the ordinary fare. He did the same on the 22nd September. For the defence, it was argued that the defendant was a workman, entitled to G12vel at workmen's rates, and in fact he did travel every night and morning by workmen's cars. On the days named he was travelling to Lofthouse Colliery for the purpose of drawing his wages. The bench decided to convict, as they considered that the defendant was neither going to work nor returning from work, as provided by the company's byelaws. They ordered him to pay 18 shillings fines and costs on the two charges, with the alternative of 14 days.

Newspaper: *Ossett Observer,* 13 October 1906

The Comfort on Long-distance Trams.

Wakefield Tramways Company Adopt a New Seat

Wakefield Tramways Company have adopted a new form of seat, known as the 'Wheeler Seat', for the inside of such of their tramcars as travel long distances – as for instance those running between Wakefield and Leeds. The Wheeler Seat is designed to give all the comfort of a cushion, without the danger of microbes and dust associated with the plush cushions seen in some tramcars. It consists of a cane-work seat and back, lined inside with canvas and supported by springs. The backs are made reversible, as in the case of the 'garden' seats, and, with their shining brass mountings and light-coloured cane straws, give a more cheerful appearance to the interior of the cars, making them reminiscent of American saloon cars. There are already twelve cars fitted with these seats, in use by the Wakefield company, but some of these are destined for the route at Castleford, which has just been opened out.

Newspaper: *Ossett Observer,* 20 October 1906

In 1908, the Wakefield & District Light Railway Company formed a subsidiary company, Lofthouse Park Limited, to build and operate an amusement park. The site was on the east side of the main road at Lofthouse Hill. The park was opened on Wednesday 3 June 1908. Amenities included a pavilion, winter gardens, skating rink, house of mirrors, maze, bandstand and gardens. Trams arrived from the Leeds and Wakefield directions to disgorge passengers at a special sidings on the opposite side of the road. At holiday times, the range of attractions was increased. From 3 to 8 August 1908, there were military band performances, open-air dances, pierrot and variety shows, including Barry Moon's Merry Mascots. Then, someone complained about having to pay 6d for a pint of beer, which was obtainable elsewhere for 1½d. By 1913, the novelty of the park was wearing thin. The large wooden pavilion at Lofthouse Park, built in a mock-oriental design, is featured above, shortly after opening. *Postcard: courtesy of Raymond Colley.*

These are reproductions of some of several postcards which were on sale at Lofthouse Park from 1908 onwards. *Postcards.*

During the 1914-18 War, Lofthouse Park became a camp for German and other internees. In 1921, it was taken over by five Lancashire businessmen, with a view to reopening. Late in the evening of Saturday, 22 April 1922, the pavilion and various ancillary buildings caught fire. Wakefield Fire Brigade refused to attend, so the Stanley Brigade made a gallant attempt to extinguish the flames. By morning, as shown, much of the complex was a tangled mass, with the chimneys remaining largely intact. The project was never resurrected. *Photograph: courtesy of Raymond Colley.*

This is the open-top West Riding tramcar which was decorated in May 1909 to celebrate Wakefield Trinity winning the Northern Union Rugby Challenge Cup. It toured the area and was illuminated at night. The team was known as 'Dreadnoughts' for many years. The Wakefield to Agbrigg trams passed close to the team's Belle Vue ground. *Postcard.*

This and the following pages trace the route of the West Riding tramway from Agbrigg to Ossett. Above, tramcar number 50 sojourns at its terminus outside the *Duke of York Hotel* in Agbrigg Road, its destination indicator set to Ossett. *Postcard: William Colin Machan, fancy goods dealer, Wakefield.*

Also seen outside the *Duke of York Hotel* is the WR works and permanent way car. It was ordered from Dick, Kerr in 1904 and had the same truck and electrical equipment as the 1-30 batch of trams. It was damaged in the 1917 depot fire at Castleford, but later rebuilt. Interestingly, this illustration, probably from the 1920s, shows an extra block of houses. But the lamp on the tram standard has vanished. Less obvious, but worthy of note, is the automatic trolley reverser, installed in about 1913. *Postcard: H M Wilson, Wood Street, Wakefield.*

An unidentified tramcar of the 1-30 batch trundles along Doncaster Road, not far from the famous rugby ground (behind the trees on the left) at Belle Vue, in about 1905. The section of wide road facilitated the use of double track. Many of the buildings shown, including the Primitive Methodist Chapel on the right, have now been demolished. *Postcard: E I Walker, Wakefield.*

With Ossett as its destination, tramcar number 67, part of the 62-67 batch, crosses Chantry Bridge, with King's Mill in the background, left. Strangely, this batch, built in 1906 by the United Electric Car Company of Preston (another subdivision of Dick, Kerr), reverted to open-top type. Top covers were fitted in 1913. Tramcar number 67 is pictured here in green livery, probably in 1925. *Postcard: J Valentine & Sons, Dundee.*

In Kirkgate, Wakefield, a white-coated traffic policeman looks quietly confident, in spite of the confluence of five roads. West Riding tramcar number 9, having passed the *Grey Horse Hotel* and negotiated the railway bridge, is about to cross Chantry Bridge and start the final leg of its journey to Agbrigg. The top cover, with three windows per side to match the lower deck, was fitted just before the Great War; here, a decade or so later, the car looks in fine condition.

Postcard: Edgar L Scrivens, Doncaster.

RING
UP
235
CROWN
LIVERY
STABLES
FOR
MOTOR
HEARSE
CARRIAGES
ETC.
FUNERAL
DIRECTOR
14. ARUNDEL ST.,
BARNSLEY
BREWERY Ld
AGBRIGG
Copyright.

WR tramcar number 55, built in 1905, is pictured in almost new condition in Wakefield's Kirkgate, on its way to Ossett. The wide road is fully setted and has double tracks. The very old building on the right, known as the *Six Chimneys*, with ground floor shops, collapsed in May 1941 and was not rebuilt. A roundabout, with subways, now occupies the area in the foreground. *Postcard: W C Machan, Wakefield.*

The *Crown & Anchor Hotel*, the *Six Chimneys* and the ornate tram standard, shown in this view from about 1910, have all vanished. This *Six Chimneys* must not be confused with a recent creation of the same name further up Kirkgate. *Postcard: H G Glen & Company, Park Lane, Leeds.*

WR tramcar number 12 descends Upper Kirkgate on its way to Agbrigg, having just passed Wakefield Cathedral. The image, from either late 1904 or early 1905, provides an interesting study in tramlines and granite setts. And just look at that pram. *Photograph: G & J Hall, Wakefield.*

Photographed in 1907, tramcar number 41 pauses on the southeastern side of the Bull Ring, not far from the grocery shop of John Charles Kay, before continuing its journey to Ossett. This was one of a number of establishments in a block which included the better-known Jessop's and Brotherton's shops. Driver, conductor and inspector proudly pose, whilst a couple of boys look set for a ride on the open balcony. *Postcard.*

Tramcar number 71 is featured in the Bull Ring, collecting passengers for its run to Agbrigg. The shops of George Jessop & Sons, clothiers, and Charles Archibald Brotherton, draper, are visible on the right. The tramcar formed part of the batch hired from Leeds City Tramways in 1917 and purchased in 1919, to replace cars lost in the Castleford fire. They were built as open-toppers in 1899 by Brush of Loughborough. Top covers were fitted at Leeds in 1913. Around Wakefield, the cars were sometimes nicknamed 'Flat-fronts', a not entirely accurate description, although the different end profile is obvious. *Postcard: J Valentine & Sons, Dundee.*

The Ossett route tramlines are seen running from the Bull Ring, by the top of Cross Square (and the fine Grand Clothing Hall building), before swinging into Westgate. *Postcard: J Valentine & Sons, Dundee.*

In the early 1920s, this waiting room and parcels office was erected for the Yorkshire (West Riding) Electric Tramways Company on the south side of Cross Square, just below Webster's Cafe. It was a couple of minutes walk from the tram stops in the Bull Ring, although, by the 1920s, some of the West Riding buses were departing from Cross Square. The waiting room survived until the bus station was opened in 1952. *Postcard.*

97 1445

1d

YORKSHIRE (W.R.) ELECTRIC TRAMS. CO. LTD.

Not Transferable. Issued subject to Co.'s Bye-laws. Available only by car and journey on which issued and to stage point indicated by punch-hole.

1		28
2		27
3		26
4		25
5		24
6		23
7		22
8		21
9		20
10		19
11		18
12		17
13		16
14		15

Bell Punch Co., Uxbridge

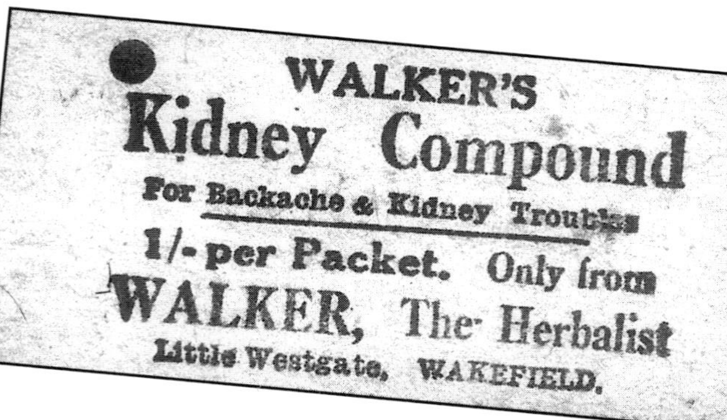

The tram conductor's tools-of-the-trade were a leather money bag, a rack of tickets, a bell-punch machine and a whistle. The hand-rack accommodated packs of pre-printed tickets of various denominations and colours. Eventually, geographical stages tended to be replaced by numerical ones. The ticket (white) on the left, with numerical stages, was issued by the West Riding Company in the 1920s. The appropriate stage was punched on the ticket machine, which gave out a pinging sound. Extra revenue was generated by allowing advertisements to appear on the backs of tickets (above). Christopher B Walker, herbalist, dispensed bottles of variously coloured and flavoured liquids from his shop at 25 Little Westgate, Wakefield.

This montage includes a view looking down Westgate. The young WR conductress, complete with money bag and whistle, looks ready to punch someones ticket, perhaps during the 1914-18 War. The Bell Punch & Printing Company of London supplied machines and tickets.

Postcard (main view): J Valentine & Sons, Dundee. Postcard (conductress): Black & White Studio, Kirkgate, Wakefield. Inset (ticket machine): advert in Motor Transport Year Book for 1929-30.

Tramcar number 70, an ex-Leeds vehicle, climbs Westgate, Wakefield, en route for Agbrigg. The short top covers on these trams meant that the stairways were exposed to the elements. The spire of Wakefield Cathedral is visible in the distance; the smaller spire nearer the camera is that of the erstwhile Wakefield Industrial Co-operative Society. The *Great Northern Hotel* on the right is a reminder of the Great Northern Railway, whose trains used Westgate Station, a little lower down on the left. *Postcard: J Valentine & Sons, Dundee.*

The trees and Georgian-style buildings are complemented by the centre-mounted tram standards with scroll patterns, in this panorama of a wide and elegant part of Westgate, looking towards Westgate Common. Tramcar number 21 proceeds on its way to Horbury and Ossett. Distant mill chimneys and piles of horse muck bring us back to reality. *Postcard: E I Walker, Wakefield.*

A very heavy snowfall at Christmas 1906 seemed especially severe in the Horbury area. Two WR tramcars are shown marooned near the Wakefield boundary, not far from the old dyehouse. Company and council workmen were brought in to clear the snow, reputed to be six feet deep in places. One tram was fitted with a snowplough. *Postcard.*

Photographed at nearly the same spot sometime later, tramcar number 11 makes its way towards Horbury and Ossett. On the reverse of this card, Auntie Lizzie, writing to nephew Jack, states, 'The cars was all lost in the snow'. *Postcard.*

With Sowood Farm in the background, WR tramcar number 22 pauses not far from the depot at South Ossett. The car is in almost new condition, but already festooned with advertisements. The driver and conductor have not been kitted with proper uniforms, which suggests a late 1904 date. *Postcard: G & J Hall, Wakefield.*

Tramcar number 47, of the 31-55 batch, is parked outsid the WR depot at Sowood Lane, Ossett. The depot, with three sets of tracks entering it was constructed to reduce dead mileage. This batch of trams was supplied in 1905, complete with top covers, and four windows per side on eac deck. Few alterations were made throughout their life. According to the message on the back of the card, posted i 1910, 'The driver is our Willie'. His surname is unknown. A notice in a lower deck window lists the towns and villages on the Sandal to Leeds route, and the destination blind is set at Leeds. This, plus the sight of a workman and his mate, possibly suggests that the tran had been sent to Ossett for a checkup. *Postcard.*

Within a few days of the official opening, tramcar number 22 is featured on roadside single track, in narrow Station Road, Ossett. In the distance, the track veers left on to the Bank Street terminus. The destination indicator is already set for the return journey. *Postcard.*

WR tramcar number 15 awaits deparure from the terminus in Bank Street, Ossett. It will shortly move forward and turn into Station Road on the right (note the wires). Most of the buildings on the left remain; those on the right have gone. Beyond the tram is the old Grammar School, demolished in 1906 to make way for the Town Hall. In 1908, the tram terminus was moved nearer to the top of Dale Street, shown to the left of the tram. *Postcard.*

Offensive Conduct on a Tramcar

'At the West Riding Court, Wakefield, yesterday, an Ossett young man named Harry Lister was charged with swearing or using abusive language while riding on a car of the Wakefield & District Light Railway Company. Mr Gerald Beaumont appeared to prosecute and stated that the offence took place on Sunday night, 27th May. Complaints had reached the offices of the company about rowdyism on cars on Sunday nights, and the traffic superintendent had put special men on to try and remedy the trouble. Defendant boarded the car at Wakefield Market Place at 9.30 and commenced by disputing the amount of the fare to the Half Way House, Horbury, which was 2½d. He ultimately paid the fare, but began to swear and use bad language, and complaints were made by some of the passengers, among them a lady. When the Half Way House was reached, he refused to get off, and rode on to two further stopping places. After he got off, he took hold of the back of the car and ran along for some time, but utimately let go. The last had not been seen of him, however, for later on, an inspector boarded the car, and when the car stopped at Horbury Road, defendent was heard running behind it. The inspector turned round and saw defendant about to strike him. The inspector asked him what was the matter, and defendant used more disgusting language. Evidence bearing out Mr Beaumont's statement was given by John North, conductor; William Clarke, inspector; Robert Fallas, colliery deputy, Springstone Avenue, Ossett; and Claude Hainsworth, butcher, Ryecroft Street, Ossett. Defendant said he never spoke a word to anybody. There were four previous convictions against defendant, and the bench fined him 8s 6d and £1 11s 6d costs, or a month, the chairman saying it was a very bad case. Newspaper: *Ossett Observer,* 16 June 1906

Tramway Money Missing

The Wakefield City Police are investigating a mysterious robbery which has occurred at the depot of the Wakefield & District Light Railway Company. About £100 has disappeared from one of the safes. Newspaper: *Ossett Observer,* 8 September 1906

Ruined by Tramways

George Cawthraw, herring curer and wagonette proprietor, of Wakefield, whose liabilities were £402, with a deficiency of £277, was examined in bankruptcy at Wakefield on Thursday.

The debtor stated that he had been in business at Wakefield for about 42 years, and at one time did fairly well. Latterly, however, trade had fallen off in both the fish and wagonette departments. People would not have salt fish now – it must be fresh – and he had had large quantities to throw away. As to the wagonette trade, it had been ruined by the advent of the tramways.

Newspaper: *Ossett Observer*, 7 July 1906

Scholars' Picnic

The annual outing for the scholars and teachers associated with the Congregational Sunday School, Westfield Road, Horbury, took place on Saturday, when a party of about 150 persons, both children and adults, visited Heath Common. The journey from Horbury to Agbrigg and back was made in two special tramcars, which started about half past two o'clock in the afternoon and returned shortly after nine in the evening. The outing was greatly enjoyed. Tea was served on Heath Common.

Newspaper: *Ossett Observer*, 21 July 1906

Wesley Guild Outing

Under the auspices of the Wesley Guild connected with the Wesley Street Church, Ossett, one of a series of rambles was arranged for Saturday afternoon to Sandal Castle. Owing to the threatening weather, only about a score of members assembled. They proceeded to Sandal by electric car, and after a short visit to the castle ruins, had tea at a cottage. Returning to Wakefield, the party inspected the Cathedral and remained to the evening service.

Newspaper: *Ossett Observer*, 18 August 1906

(Although not stated, the party probably changed trams in Wakefield on the outward as well as the return journey).

Trap Accident

An accident caused by the wheels of a trap catching in the tramlines has occurred at Wakefield. Mr Thomas Hallas, carting agent, Outwood, and his wife, were driving up Northgate, and the trap was thrown over, and the occupants pitched into the road. They were taken into a house and, having been attended by a doctor, were able to proceed home.

Newspaper: *Ossett Observer*, 1 September 1906

From early October 1906 onwards, some West Riding tramcars were withdrawn from the Wakefield system to serve the Castleford area. They were taken on low loaders, pulled by steam traction engines, from Rothwell Haigh Depot to Castleford Depot. (At Wakefield, the displaced cars were replaced by slightly newer ones). The Board of Trade inspection was carried out on 20 October 1906, starting at Normanton. Excited children are pictured lining the end of the town's High Street as tramcar number 29 begins its inspection run to Castleford and Pontefract. *Postcard.*

The same tramcar, number 29, is seen entering Pontefract Road, Castleford, later that day. Children, who had probably never experienced a tram before, are trying to keep up with it. The bowler-hatted dignitaries, visible on the top deck, plus other guests, were served with lunch in Pontefract, after which the car and party returned to Normanton via Castleford. Major Pringle, the Board of Trade inspector, approved the tramway. *Postcard.*

Thursday, 25 October 1906 was the date of the formal opening ot the Castleford area tramways. Several tramcars, some of them decorated, carried specially invited guests. Here, a pair of trams, having just left the nearby depot on Wheldon Road, Castleford, stand in front of the *Ship Inn* at Bridge Foot, an area where local people assembled for parades and public meetings. An entirely male contingent looks on, whilst ladies and gentlemen, dressed in their finery, board the cars. *Postcard.*

On the same day, 25 October, the tradesmen's reserved car gets a tumultuous send-off from the terminus at the end of Normanton's High Street. On the right are the shops of Carr the chemist and Alfred Blakeley the draper. *Postcard.*

West Riding tramcar number 30 rests at the Normanton terminus on the end of High Street and at the edge of the Market Place in about 1908. The car later received a top cover and was one of several trams returned to Wakefield after the Castleford lines closed. *Postcard: Newland Series.*

Tramcar number 29, in Pontefract's Corn Market, nears the end of its journey from Normanton and Castleford in around 1910. The wide and setted road is flanked by several picturesque hostelries. The town was famous for its liquorice growing and refining. *Postcard: J Valentine & Sons, Dundee.*

Tramcar number 18 approaches the terminus in Pontefract's Market Place, its indicator already set for the return journey. The photograph probably dates from the 1914-18 War or after. The car appears to be in one of the emergency liveries introduced because of paint shortages during that war – possibly dark green or brown. *Postcard.*

The Normanton-Castleford-Pontefract route was mainly single track with passing loops, although double track was laid at the two extremities and along Oxford Street in Castleford. At Pontefract, the double track extended over Front Street, Corn Market, Beast Fair and Market Place. The latter is depicted here in about 1912.

The splendour of the buildings, including the Market Hall at middle left and the Town Hall in the distance, is carried through to the tram standards with their ornamental scrollwork. Although some road traffic is evident, and a tram could swing round the corner at any minute, the two fashionably-dressed ladies in the foreground seem to be in no danger. *Postcard: W Bramley, Cross Gates.*

NORMANTON
HOTEL
U-9133

Left: West Riding tramcar number 11 (or possibly 21) waits at the Pontefract terminus, near the *Elephant Hotel* to the right, before departing for Normanton. This is one of several cars transferred from Wakefield to Castleford after the latter's 1917 depot fire. The lower notice visible on the tram platform reads, 'No dogs allowed inside this car', whilst a sign higher up includes, 'No standing on car platforms'. *Postcard.*

Above: The tram route from Pontefract to Castleford skirted Pontefract Park and Racecourse. The tramway company benefitted from the extra revenue accrued from race days and other special events held in the park. Here, on a quieter day in about 1907, tramcar number 23, having just traversed the long Park Road and negotiated a passing loop, is proceeding towards Pontefract. To the left is one of a pair of matching gatehouses at the entrance to the park and course. *Postcard.*

Below: This top-covered tramcar, from the 31-55 batch, was ingeniously decorated to encourage people to shop in Pontefract. It toured the area, but is pictured here in Pontefract Market Place, with the *Elephant Hotel* on the left. *Postcard.*

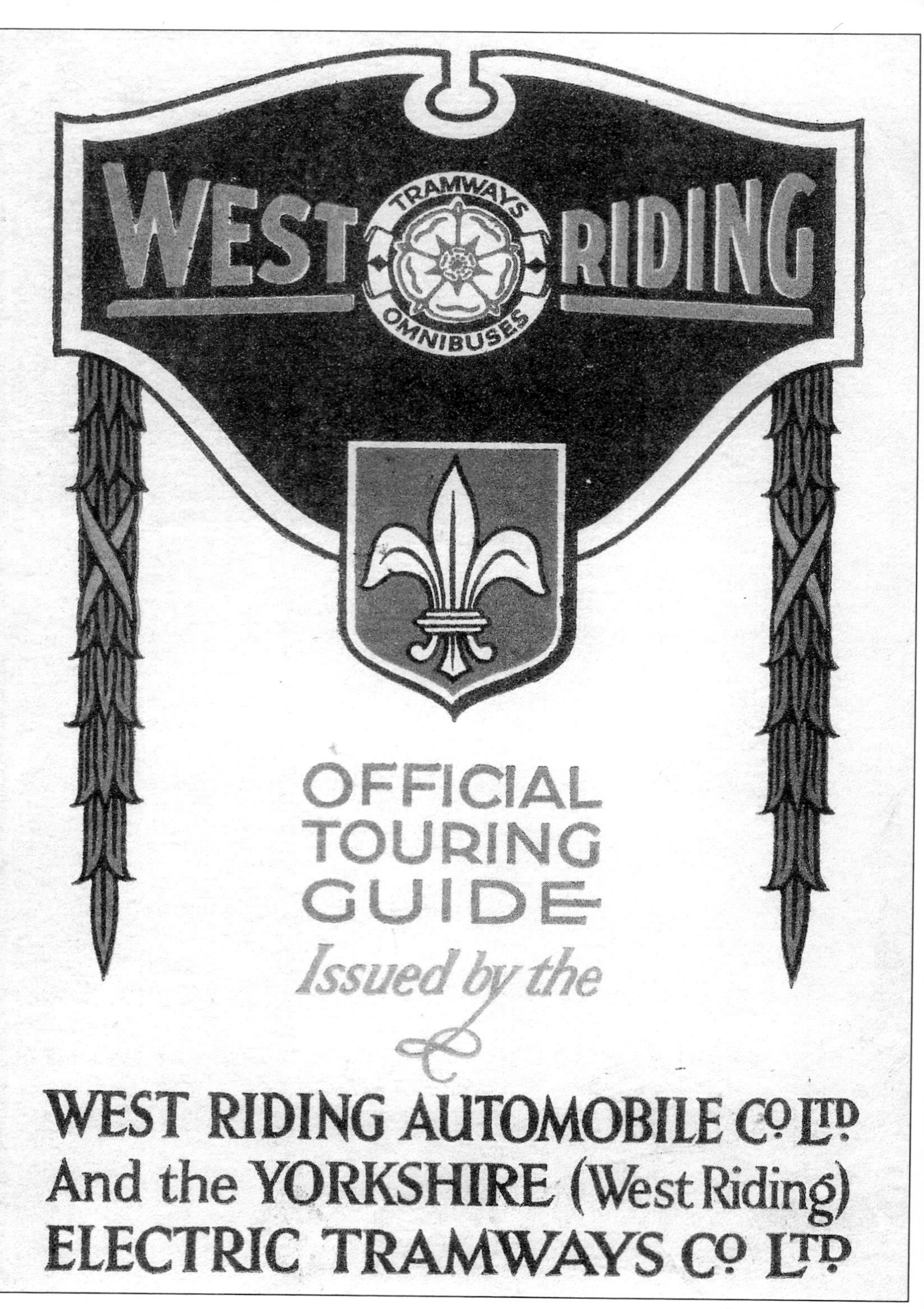

The West Riding Company published a number of touring guides. The front cover of the third edition, released in 1927, is reproduced above. This cover, in buff, brown and blue (decidedly not company colours!) shows the West Riding rose emblem, introduced in 1924, and carried on the sides of trams and buses. The 148 pages include details of places to visit, although no precise details on how to get there are included. *Booklet.*

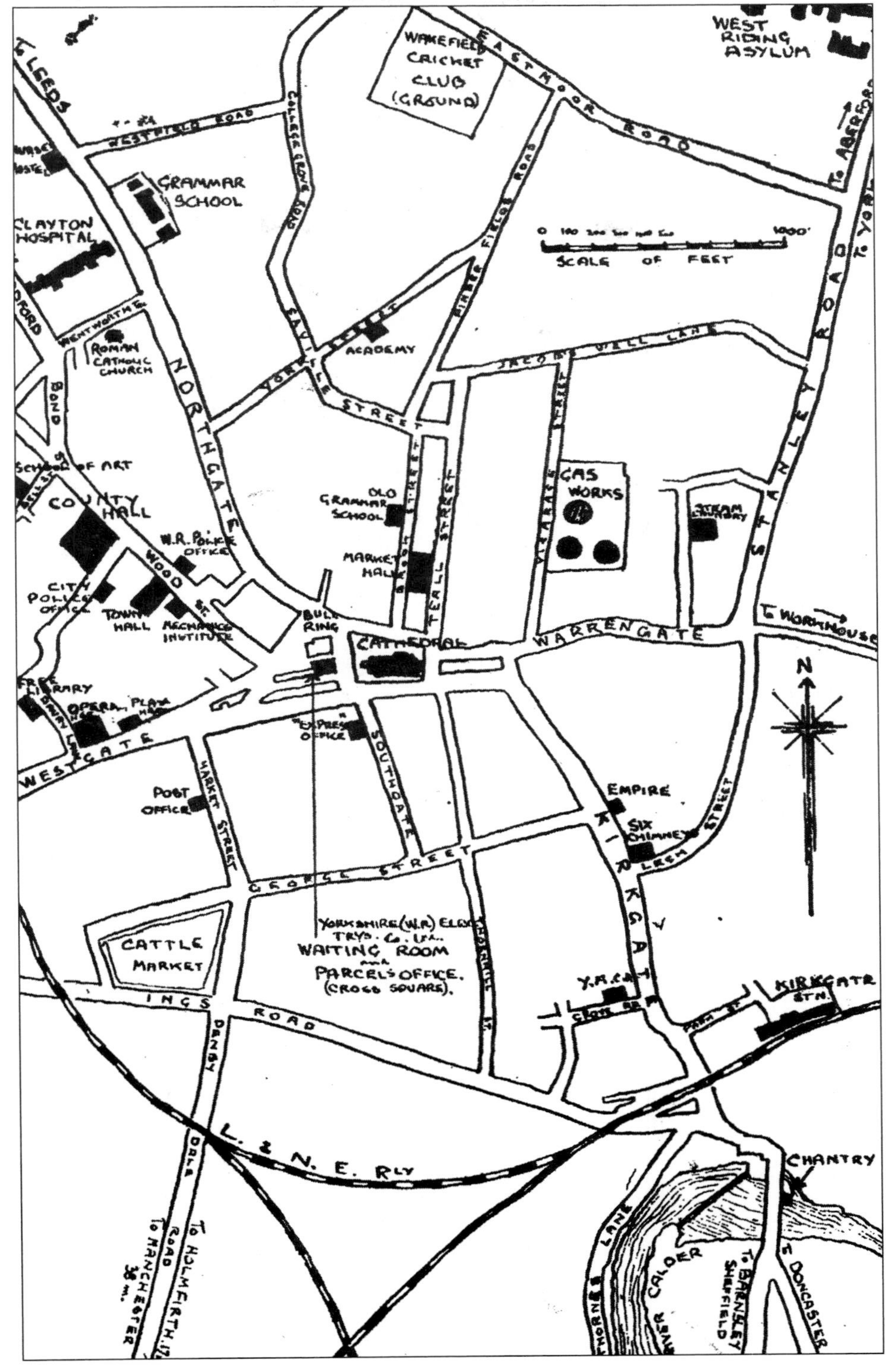

This map is taken from the 1927 West Riding Official Touring Guide. It shows the roads traversed by WR trams through Wakefield, including Chantry Bridge, Kirkgate, Upper Kirkgate, Bull Ring and Northgate (and on to Leeds). Part of Westgate is also depicted (in the direction of Horbury and Ossett). *Booklet.*

Of the three West Riding Tramway Company routes, the last to close was Agbrigg to Ossett. No special ceremony was held, the final day of operation being Monday, 25 July 1932. However, a few photographers did turn out. Reputed to be the last tramcar, number 60, is featured on these two photographs, taken on the western side of Horbury, not far from the depot at Sowood, Ossett. This tram, new in 1906, had remained largely unaltered, except for livery changes and a motor upgrade. On one of the pictures, the conductor is holding his rack of tickets. Next day, the Ossett-Agbrigg trams were replaced by new red West Riding double-deck centre-entrance Leyland Titan buses of the type which had recently displaced trams on the Leeds-Sandal and Leeds-Rothwell routes. The three routes were affectionately dubbed 'the track' for years after. *Photographs.*

CHAPTER 4

Dewsbury, Ossett & Soothill Nether Tramways

On high ground, two miles east of Dewsbury, the town of Ossett became distinguished for the production of mungo and shoddy in a number of small and medium-sized textile mills. Although the Yorkshire Woollen District trams permeated to the west, north and south of Dewsbury, no progress had materialized eastwards towards Ossett. The notoriously steep 'cutting', which passed through Earlsheaton, may have been a deterrent. Ossett was tolerably well-served by the Great Northern Railway, whose Wakefield-Dewsbury line incorporated stations at Ossett, Earlsheaton and Flushdyke. A spur from Ossett to Batley included a station at Chickenley Heath.

The Wakefield & District Light Railway Company had applied in 1901 for powers to construct a tramway from Wakefield to Dewsbury, passing through Ossett, and with a branch to Earlsheaton. The GNR, plus the Lancashire & Yorkshire Railway, whose line from Wakefield to Dewsbury took a more southerly course, immediately objected. The application for a tramway received support from the Mayor of Ossett, Councillor Walter Townend, and some of the Ossett ratepayers. However, the powers were allowed to lapse.

The National Electric Construction Company, which had originated in 1897, became the second largest tramway syndicate in Britain, but it was much smaller than the British Electric Traction Company (of which the YWD was part). It decided to negotiate with three local authorities, including Ossett, with a view to tramway operation. Although the discussions were somewhat protracted, the three proposed tramways were authorised in the *Dewsbury Corporation Tramways Order* 1904, the *Ossett Corporation Tramways Order* 1904 and the *Soothill Nether Urban District Tramways Act* 1904. The whole would be operated as one entity. (Soothill Nether is the old name for Earlsheaton).

The three authorities were to own the tramway, but the construction of track and overhead equipment was carried out by the National Electric Construction Company. The greatest length was owned by Soothill Nether, the shortest by Dewsbury. Construction of the tramway dragged on, causing exasperation to local residents, particularly those living on the north side of Ossett. The tramway, known as the Dewsbury Ossett & Soothill Nether Tramways, was leased back to the NEC. The title was later altered to the Dewsbury & Ossett Tramways.

The tramway was largely single track with passing loops. The Dewsbury end terminated near the Town Hall, at the eastern side of the Market Place. From there, the track climbed the steep hill out of the town, ran along Wakefield Road, passed through Chickenley Heath, and approached the centre of Ossett by traversing Church Street. In Ossett, a junction was made with the Yorkshire (West Riding) Electric Tramway (covered in the previous chapter). Part way up the cutting from Dewsbury, a spur was constructed along High Road and Town Street into Earlsheaton. Part of the road through Earlsheaton had to be widened. A proposal to continue the tramway along Syke Lane, to join the track on Wakefield Road, was abandoned.

By late October 1908, trial runs were being made over the system. Representatives of the three local authorities seemed to be satisfied. The official Board of Trade inspection was carried out on 11 November. Two decorated tramcars were provided for the opening ceremony on 12 November. Public service commenced on the following day. Two separate services were run: Dewsbury Market Place to Ossett Market Place; and Dewsbury Market Place to Earlsheaton. On the Ossett route, an initial slightly erratic service settled down to one of ten minute intervals throughout most of the weekday period. The service to and from Earlsheaton was every twenty minutes, although this was augmented to ten minutes on Dewsbury's market days. Drastic curtailment of services occurred during the 1914-18 War, due to employees being called up.

The Dewsbury & Ossett Tramways operated slightly more than three miles of route. The depot, in Church Street, Ossett, eventually housed twelve double-deck tramcars, all of them initially open-topped. The first batch, numbers 1 to 8, were delivered in 1908 from Brush of Loughborough. They arrived at Ossett Station, from where they were taken on low loaders to Church Street. Four further trams were acquired second-hand from the Mexborough & Swinton Tramway Company (also part of the National Electric Construction Company), two being delivered in 1911 and two in 1928.

By the late 1920s, there was talk of replacing Ossett's trams with buses. Even trolleybuses were seriously considered. A new road, called Kingsway, was opened in 1928 from Streetside (near Chickenley Heath) to the centre of Ossett, which offered potential for a slightly shorter bus-operated route from Dewsbury to Ossett. The Dewsbury & Ossett Tramways were taken over by the Yorkshire (Woollen District) Electric Tramways Company, which was itself becoming committed to a tram replacement scheme. The final D&O trams ran on Sunday 19 October 1933. In late evening, a crowd assembled in Ossett Market Place to wave goodbye to a packed last tram as it headed for the depot in Church Street. Next day, YWD buses took over.

The formal opening of the Dewsbury, Ossett & Soothill Nether Tramways on the afternoon of 12 November 1908 was marked by the decoration of a pair of tramcars, numbers 2 and 3. These carried invited members of the three participating local authorities on a tour of the system. The Mayor of Ossett drove one car to the Chickenley Heath boundary, where the Chairman of Soothill Nether Urban District Council assumed control, until the Dewsbury border was reached when their Town Clerk took over. The two cars are pictured, together with officials and associates of the various local authorities. Most of them are bowler-hatted, although a few cloth caps are in evidence. *Postcard.*

On 12 November 1908, one of the two decorated tramcars is greeted by local residents at the Earlsheaton terminus in Town Street. *Postcard.*

A Dewsbury & Ossett tramcar of the 1-8 batch, having emerged from Church Street, travels up Dale Street, Ossett, on the last part of its journey from Dewsbury. The old Ossett Co-operative Society buildings are on the left. On the right is the *Horse & Jockey Inn.* *Postcard.*

Dewsbury & Ossett tramcar number 2, part of the 1 to 8 batch, stands in Church Street, Ossett, near the company's depot. This batch of trams was built by the Brush Electrical Engineering Company of Loughborough in 1908. They were to a standard Brush design, supplied also to other subsidiaries of the National Electric Construction Company. The fitting of top covers did not commence until 1915. The trams seated twenty-two passengers inside on longitudinal seats and thirty-two outside on transverse ones. The between-deck stairs were of half-turn direct spiral type. Destination boxes were suspended from the canopy above the driver's head. Two swan-neck lighting standards were fitted on the upper deck. The original livery of the D&O trams was dark red and off-white. The waist panels were lined out to create three rectangles, the centre one carrying a garter with the full title of Dewsbury, Ossett & Soothill Nether Tramways. After the 1914-18 War, the livery was changed to maroon and off-white and Dewsbury & Ossett Tramways was spelt out along the length of the waist panel. The names on the caps of the uniformed staff, who also feature on the above picture, are 'conductor', 'motorman' and 'inspector' respectively. 'Motorman' was another name for a tram driver. The windows of the car are well plastered with notices, at least two of them advertising the Ossett Show.
Postcard: Mark Cross, Dewsbury.

Dewsbury & Ossett tramcar number 6 stands outside the depot in Church Street with a pair of company employees. Note the adverts. E P Shaw's dry ginger ale came from their works in Wakefield. Charles White's bakery was in Daisy Hill, Dewsbury. *Postcard: Mark Cross, Dewsbury.*

This is the same tramcar, number 6, as shown on the previous page (confirmed by the same location, same adverts and part of the fleet number). A pair of inspectors grace the photograph. Track can be seen running off towards the depot yard on the right. *Postcard: Mark Cross, Dewsbury.*

An initial proposal to route the Dewsbury & Ossett tramcars from Dewsbury Road along the whole length of Dale Street and into Ossett Market Place was abandoned in favour of Church Street, which meant that only a short length of Dale Street was used. The depot was built in Church Street, as was the adjacent Yorkshire Electric Power Company's sub-station, from which the D&O obtained its power. This illustration depicts the depot on Church Street in the early 1930s. By then, the tramcars, which began life with open upper decks, had received top covers. Those shown are from the 1 to 8 batch. A large proportion of the staff is featured. The cap insignias show 'inspector', 'motorman' and 'conductor'. On the back row, at extreme left under the Ossett destination sign, is Mr Shadlock, a motorman. The group of workpeople also includes: Messrs B Audsley, T Bragg, L Farnhill, H Gothard, H Jackson, P Newsome, H Noble, Ramsden, D Stones, E Sugden, Warburton, B Willans and Mrs Senior. Mr P Newsome was employed as a painter. The car sheds have had a variety of uses since 1933, including storage facilities for the Woodhead Manufacturing Company, whose factory stood opposite in Church Street. *Postcard.*

The D&O tramway depot is again shown in the early 1930s, but this time with cars numbers 10 (left) and 9 (right). These trams had been constructed by Brush in 1906. After service with the Mexborough & Swinton Tramway Company, they were sold in open-top condition to the D&O in 1911, numbered into their fleet, and later given top covers. Numbers 9 and 10 were similar in most respects to numbers 1 to 8. However, they had a slightly less overall height, and the stair rails ended by being joined to a vertical stanchion on the lower deck, instead of being looped. Two further cars were bought from the M&S in 1928, becoming numbers 11 and 12. These Brush built open-toppers had acquired top covers some years before. *Postcard: Mark Cross, Dewsbury.*

This 1930 view of Church Street, Ossett, shows a passing loop and the type of side pole, with a small scroll design, which was used on the Dewsbury & Ossett system. The tram is quite near the depot, located on the right-hand side of the road. *Postcard.*

A tramcar of the 1-8 batch, having left Church Street, heads along Dewsbury Road at Streetside, on its way to Dewsbury. At this point, the wiring is shown to be span type, suspended from side poles, with the small scroll design. *Postcard: James Edward Shaw, stationer, Ossett.*

The tram track and wiring poles are seen disappearing into the distance on this vista of High Road, Earlsheaton, from about 1930. Interspersed with the tram standards are telegraph poles. Part of the setted road has been tarmacked. Partially hidden on the left (near the cyclist) is the now-demolished Wesleyan Chapel. Earlsheaton was a thriving community, with its own schools, pubs, shops and mills. The remote siting of the railway station did not suit everyone, so the trams appropriated some of the local passenger business. *Postcard: E & H Rigg, Post Office, Earlsheaton.*

From a high vantage point, the terminus of the Dewsbury & Ossett trams is featured outside Dewsbury Town Hall, on the right, in 1915. On the left is the erstwhile and much lamented Empire Theatre. The Town Hall is decorated for a wartime recruiting campaign. However, the crowds have gathered for a religious festival in the Town Hall, including a contingent from Highfield Congregational Chapel at Earlsheaton. Tramcar number 3 is filling up for Ossett, but nobody seems to want the Earlsheaton car. It was customary for the Earlsheaton and Ossett trams to leave at the same time. The tramlines are shown disappearing behind the Town Hall and up the notorious cutting, where, over the years, various vehicles came to grief. *Photograph.*

A pair of D&O tramcars stand at their Dewsbury terminus, with the Lancashire & Yorkshire Bank in the background on the right. The crowds have gathered for a military display on 26 June 1915. The farthest tram, either number 9 or 10, carries patriotic flags and recruitment posters. *Postcard: Fred Hartley, Dewsbury.*

A charabanc in front of Dewsbury Town Hall awaits departure on an afternoon tour. A D&O tramcar rests at its terminus. Behind the charabanc, the building with the gable end is where errant tram number 3 embedded itself, after cascading down the cutting and overrunning the terminus. *Postcard.*

A Dewsbury & Ossett tramcar of the 1-8 batch stands at Dewsbury terminus in its final form, with maroon and off-white livery. The terminus had been moved to the roadside beside the bank. *Photograph.*

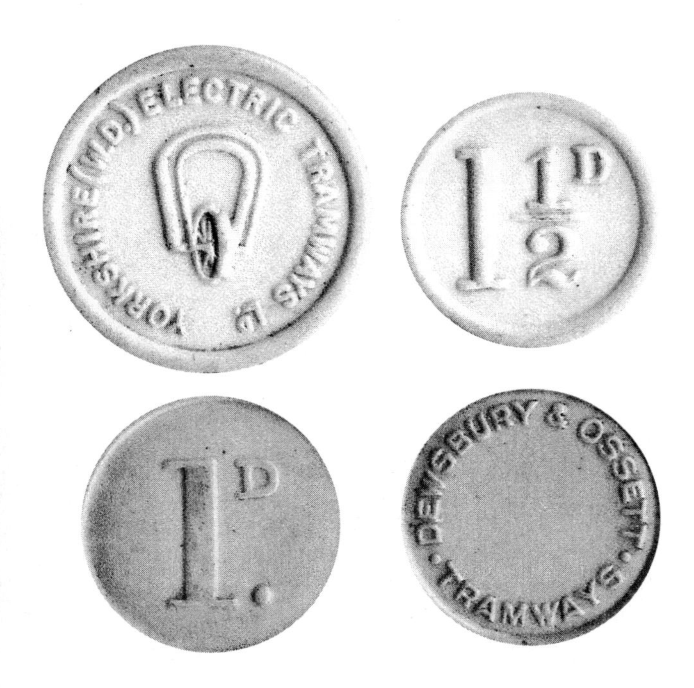

The Yorkshire Woollen and Dewsbury & Ossett companies are known to have used plastic tokens, approximately 7/8″ (22mm) in diameter. They were issued to certain school children and workers, for example postmen. The two faces of the YWD 1½d token, white in colour, and with the BET magnet-and-wheel device, are shown at the top. Underneath is the 1d yellow D&O token. An identical dark red version was also used.

A number of accidents, some of them minor, occurred on the Dewsbury & Ossett tramway system. Several tramcars overran the terminus near Dewsbury Town Hall (and trams were not the only vehicles to plummet down the steep hills around Dewsbury). A compulsory tram stop was introduced at Rishworth Street, behind the Town Hall, so that the driver could check the brakes before arriving at the actual terminus. But, on 12 October 1915, a serious accident did occur, involving tramcar number 3, which, like all the D&O cars, incorporated three kinds of brakes – hand wheel brake, mechanical brake and rheostatic brake. Tramcar number 3, the 4.15 pm from Earlsheaton, went out of control after entering the half-mile 1 in 12 gradient of Wakefield Road and began to gain speed. Near Rishworth Street, it collided with a pony and flat cart, which knocked over two women. The conductress jumped off the car beside the Town Hall and was later taken to Dewsbury Infirmary. The car bumped into a horse and cart, causing the cart to spin round and injure a man. The tramcar then overran the terminus, sped across the setts and embedded itself in Hilton's shoe shop, as pictured. A fire broke out, but was soon extinguished by the local brigade. The three passengers on the car escaped with shock. A crowd soon gathered, as did several cameramen, probably making this the most photographed tram accident in Britain. At 5.30 pm, shortly after the above photograph was taken, the upper storeys of the building, which were used by the adjoining *Scarborough Hotel*, collapsed on to the tramcar. *Postcard: Fred Hartley, Dewsbury.*

The extent of the damage to D&O tramcar number 3, also to the property after it collapsed, is well captured on this image. Observe the upturned table. *Postcard: Mark Cross, Dewsbury.*

The wall was shored up to prevent further collapse, as pictured here. The tramcar was taken back to the depot at Ossett. The driver, John James Callaghan, was questioned at the Board of Trade enquiry in November. It emerged that the rails had been in a greasy condition, probably caused by a combination of coal dust from the nearby Ridings Colliery and a shower of rain. The driver had applied the brakes, also some sand, but claimed he was unable to halt the car. After the Great War, the tramcar was repaired, fitted with a covered top and placed back in service. *Postcard: E Sykes.*

Acknowledgements & Sources

W Pickles, *The Tramways of Dewsbury and Wakefield,* Light Rail Transit Association, 1980.
J C Gillham and R J S Wiseman, *The Tramways of West Yorkshire,* Light Rail Transit Association, 2001.
Wakefield Historical Society Journal, Volume 3, 1976.
Newspapers:
Batley News
Dewsbury Reporter
Ossett Observer
Wakefield Express
Kelly's Directories.
Ordnance Survey Maps.

Postcards and photographs are credited individually if their origination is known. The following photographers deserve special mention:
Fred Hartley, Dewsbury.
Mark Cross, Dewsbury.
George & John Hall, Wakefield.
Edwin I Walker, Wakefield.
Herbert Myers Wilson, Wakefield. (Successor to Walker).

Index

General